Staying in the Game

Staying in the Game

Daily Encouragement to Keep You From Giving Up

Dr. Laura Sparks

Dr Laura Sparks.com

CONTENTS

Introduction	1
1 Sick to Death	4
2 Discover Your Genius	20
3 Avoiding Pain	40
4 Relishing Pleasure	57
5 Who Are Your People?	74
6 What is Your Why?	90
7 Steps For Today	106
8 Steps For Tomorrow	124
9 Gut Check: Getting Super Honest	142
10 Setting Goals	157
Don't Stop...	172
ABOUT THE AUTHOR	174

Copyright © 2022 by Dr. Laura Sparks

All rights reserved. No part of this book may be reproduced in any manner whatsoever without written permission except in the case of brief quotations embodied in critical articles and reviews.

First Printing, 2022

Introduction

This book is for Doers and Makers of all shapes and sizes and all walks of life. And while you may not have all the steps figured out to successfully finish your race, you have a driving passion to complete your mission. You are tired of playing small.

If you are ready to take the leap, take small steps, or just gather strength to continue meandering, I promise you that being *in motion* is necessary for both the first and last steps of your journey. And that is the good news.

So, let's assume that you have a viable idea and you have actually begun something. Perhaps it is just the smallest of beginnings. Maybe you are thinking that it is so dismal a start, that it will never or could never really, go anywhere. I can tell you, I have been there, too. I have tried and failed and walked away for long stretches. And while I may not have all the answers, I have learned that showing up is 50% of your success. S*taying in the Game* is the other, and equally necessary 50%.

I want to encourage you from a very fallible and humble place. See, when something truly grabs you enough to begin it, you can rightly take your place with 'the starters'. You have done real hard work to get here. Congratulations!

If you have *started*, it is your responsibility to see it through. And that, my friend, is the essence of this book: Encouragement for your journey, to help you see it through.

We will spend some time discovering your genius, looking into how we avoid pain and relish pleasure and how that can help or hinder goal attainment. We will spend some time honing in on your people, *your why*, steps for today and tomorrow. We will get brutally honest and set some big goals...all while learning how to enjoy the journey.

Written in short chapters, easily digestible in bite-sized pieces, one per day for 12 weeks, with the idea you will have *stayed in the game* long enough to finish your project. Long enough to prove to yourself and the world that you are playing for keeps.

There are open-response questions at the end of each day. I encourage you to take the time to answer them. If you really want to get to the core of what is holding you back, take these questions seriously. Do the work and see how much work you can get done.

My goal is to give you all the self-help, motivation and inspiration you need to keep moving forward. Will you join me and get to work?

No pressure, really, but your life is depending on it.

Scripture Quotations are from the *New International Version* of the Bible.

STAYING IN THE GAME

1

Sick to Death

If you picked up this book, you have become aware that it is time for a change. Maybe you have set goals and then you've forgotten about them. You may have even set some firm resolutions, only to have broken them within weeks or months of the initial commitment. You may have started, only to give up before you made any appreciable progress. Maybe you are sick to death of the unkept promises to yourself and know that it is high time to get in gear and do something!

I want you to know that I have been there. I have made so many excuses that I finally began to *believe* them. And in the process, I denied myself any chance to finish anything. And that is just one of the reasons we are here.

The actual goal of this book is to help you hit your goals. It is really that simple. I know that if you can *stay in the game* long enough, you are going to make something happen. And then, rather than sitting on your laurels, hit them again and again and again. I am convinced if you can do it once, you can and will do it again.

I know that you have this in you.

Let's do this...

Day 1 - Why is This so Important, Anyway?

I am a firm believer that you were born for a reason, a very distinct purpose. And that purpose, that reason, will never get accomplished unless you hang in there and *Stay in the Game.*

I have spent countless hours avoiding my own best work, with the busyness of life. It is infinitely easier to do more laundry, wipe the counter again or wander into the kitchen to peer into the refrigerator for a snack.

"But, I'm hungry!" You may argue.

Yes, I am certain that you are. However, I will argue that the hunger you feel is not a hunger for the physical, temporal food in the fridge. I contend, I will go as far as guarantee, that when you lose yourself in something that you truly love, something that truly engages your spirit, you will transcend such mundane things like physical hunger.

I am also convinced that the hunger to accomplish that big dream or goal is as importantas the physical, bodily hunger that we find ourselves distracted by. And that, if you continue to deny and ignore the gnawing need to create, a very important part of you, will surely die.

That dreamy, hope-filled part of your spirit will begin to wither away, starved for attention and nourishment. As a result, we get sick...though, not necessarily physically. We become sick of our excuses, sick of not accomplishing our goals, sick, quite frankly, of ourselves. Like ingrown toenails that have too much potential energy and nowhere to go, we fester on the inside until this gnawing is our spirit become impossible to ignore.

At this point, we have a choice. We can continue to ignore our greatest needs and desires for meaningful contribution, taking us down, deeper into denial. Or, we can choose to get into that creative work that is tugging at the deepest parts of us. Clearly, the longer we let this go, the harder it will be to pull ourselves out, or break our our established habits. And the harder it will be to bounce back.

For so many reasons, we know that this "doing nothing" is simply just not the best choice. While it may seem easier in the short run, to stop fostering our creativity and pushing through towards our dreams and goals, we are definitely not creating long term happiness.

So, today, I dare you to make the choice to seek out your purpose. I dare you to distill down your reason for being here on this planet. This "work" may not be the same thing that you do for a living, although that would be convenient. The thing that makes your heart sing, that lifts you up when you are down, that special thing that you can do with no regard, or a blatant disregard, to time. This is the thing, *this* is your jam, the game that you, must not, for the life of you, ever quit.

Your creative work, that thing that you were we were created to do, is still out there, patiently waiting for you us to come back.

It is for *that thing* that rest of this book was written...
Welcome home

1. What is an activity that you do that defies any concept of time...Something where you can while away hours, happily, and have no idea where the time went?
2. What do people who know you well, think you are especially skilled at?
3. What do you want to be remembered for?

Day 2 – Paralysis by Analysis

How many times have you given up or wanted to, simply because it the task at hand was just too hard? We have the best idea ever, we toss it around, we discuss it with our spouse, friends, family. They caution us, question us and look at us with blatant skepticism. We learn about all the things that we need to be careful of, things that will 'need to be paid attention to.. The more we analyze it, the smaller the idea gets. We effectively suck the life out of it…by our very own scrutiny.

While it is always serves you to take time to make some important decisions before you begin, when you overanalyze and effectively paralyze your progress, you are not doing yourself or your project any favors. We have all been there. We have all set goals, ignored them and avoided doing certain things. And ended up with more frustration, more angst, and little or no progress to show for it..

Eventually, though, I began to learn a few things about staying in the game.

Those who successfully complete things, though, spend years setting goals and missing, re-setting, and re-adjusting, but staying in it, no matter what. If you are going hard after a goal, this will give you encouragement. If you picked this book up to learn how to hang in there, you are in the right place. If you are doing it right, there will be mishaps and missteps, messes, and chaos.

I have written and re-written this manuscript so many times, I thought I would go mad and then following some software problems, re-written one more time. I am a fellow sojourner, who, just like you, wants to play big, but finds herself repeatedly hijacked by the mundane tasks that seem to zap my time and energy.

So, why in the world do I want to stay in this game? Why do any of us want to persist at all costs? No matter what the game, we soldier on for the sake of the payoff. We know that at the end of all the hard work, it will be worth it.

There actually comes a time when all the thinking and planning leads to action. There comes a time when we have to trust ourselves and just go to work. And then, when the action is taken, trust that it is the right action and not second-guess it. This is our work.

So, if like me, you are tired of playing small, I feel your frustration and your urgency. If like me, you find yourself shunted repeatedly, even daily, by mundane tasks, your willingness to let all those other things creep in, might be sucking the life out of your efforts. It is time to trust yourself and the process. It is time for you.

1. What goal are you spending too much time thinking about?
2. Can you take a leap and just do it?
3. What is your next logical step?
4. Can you take that step today? Why or Why not?

Day 3 - Wait, What?...Without Losing My Mind?

It is possible to achieve the most important goals of your life without losing yourself or losing your mind. In fact, I will argue that unless you decide to follow hard after the most important goals in your life, you very well could. Lose your mind, that is.

It really *is* that important, and yes...life really is that crazy-making. I have spent most of my adult life serving people and helping my husband serve people. Mostly, it felt good and right. I know that I do good work at the clinic, and I really do love helping people. I have been blessed beyond measure with the skills to do my job and the ambition to stay in that game, even when it is tough.

Other than the physical demands on my body, which are significant, the work itself, as a chiropractor, is quite lovely. People get great results and usually feel better when they leave. There is nothing inherently wrong with the work, it is very rewarding and even enjoyable. And I do love helping my husband. Being there for him, supporting him, being close to him, intimately understanding the stressors that he is under, all of that makes me feel like I am serving him at the highest level. I am kind of proud that I have not slacked off in any way, at any time, and yes, admittedly, even to my own detriment.

This is also where I may have gone wrong.

When my own personal goals got hard, emotionally taxing, I think I have naturally defaulted to *his*. I have let his goals supersede my own. He never directly asked me to do this, but I have let his crises become mine. I have tended his garden first, while mine went completely neglected. I have sacrificed for the clinic, over and over again. I did it altruistically, with the best of intentions. Unfortunately, as a result, I may have starved my spirit in the process.

By neglecting the other things, like my writing, (and even my health at times!) I have communicated to myself exactly where those things sit on my own priority list. Ultimately, where I sit on my own priority list. As a result, I sometimes feel orphaned, alone, spent, and wasted.

No matter what we have accomplished together, and this has *actually* been substantial at times, I don't always feel accomplished. Because my personal goals have been placed on the back burner, I can feel at times, like I am going nowhere. Of course, it was important to help him and all the people.

What I am learning the hard way, though, is that it does not serve me to make his goals more important than mine. I have to fight for the right to my own legacy and my own work.

I am proud to say that I am currently digging myself, and my sanity, out. I am also digging my heart out of the debris. I am learning how very important it is to choose me. No, not for a mani-pedi or a massage, although those things can be a wonderful treat. I am choosing *me* by writing this. I am choosing *me*, by acknowledging my goals as important and necessary.

Whether anyone listens or reads this, I need to speak my truth. And so do you.

Just today, I heard an author say that if we have a burning drive to do something, write something, create something, *we* simply must do it. We must follow through in the moment. It is very likely that our goals and drives, over time, will change. And if we do not act in the moment, we will surely lose a very important opportunity, and then the idea, the drive, and the desire may just float away in the wind.

I think that in order to keep our sanity, we either have to pursue the driving passion, or simply let it go. It is nearly impossible to hold both in tension. I think that if we keep the goal and do nothing about it, there is a very good chance we will drive ourselves to insanity. Likewise, if we give up on the goal entirely, we may lose a bit of our sanity to that.

So, yes, it is possible to do follow your heart, to pursue your creative genius, and do this without losing your mind. In fact, it is quite imperative that you do, so that you won't.

1. What do you want to do more than anything, but find yourself avoiding.avoiding?
2. Think about the last time you had a bit of free time. What did you do with it?
3. How can you capture all those bits of free time, and harness them for the sake of your goals?

Day 4 – So, What if I Don't Create?

Yesterday, we talked about capturing the bits of time and harnessing them for the sake of your goals. You may have even made some decisions around that. Taken control of your calendar, and come up with a viable plan. And if you did, hats off to you!

Today, though, I want to address this: What if you don't? What if you just simply let that burning desire go? What if you decide that this creative pursuit is simply too hard? That it is simply not worth the fight. That you would be quite okay if you left that passion smolder and fizzle until there is absolutely no spark, and no fire. Is that really what you truly, actually want? Only you can answer that.

A good way to think about this if you project yourself 5 or 10 years into the future. Would you be happy, contented and fulfilled to have let this one go? If you can honestly say that you would be okay with letting it go 5 or 10 years from now, then it is the right decision for you.

Clearly, for most of us, the answer is a resounding, unequivocal nooooo! For most of us, the trouble is not so much being clear about our goals, the trouble is being willing to do the hard work to get to the other side. And that hard work includes choosing this goal over another one. Choosing the work over the fun. Choosing the work over the Netflix. Choosing you over whatever obligations have you distracted.

Today, I worked at the office, did dishes (twice), a load of laundry and really wanted to sit down to the recreation of the 1500 piece jigsaw puzzle on my dining room table. Instead, I am here and I am writing. I am stealing this time away because I know that after this chapter is finished, I will feel like I accomplished something. Something important for me. I also realize, each time I sit down to this, how very much I love the actual work of it! In some ways, it is every bit as fun as the jigsaw puzzle. Maybe more so.

Too many times, I think we choose everything else first because we forget that stealing even a few moments away today, in an effort to accomplish our goals, will bring us closer to achieving them tomorrow.

Capitalizing on that little bit of time, will keep you focused, on track and moving forward in the direction of your dreams. No matter how small it might seem.

1. In 5 years, picture where you want to be and journal your thoughts.
2. Do the same for where you want to be 10 years from now.
3. What can you do today that will move you in that direction?

Day 5 – Healing

Baby Steps. Small bits of progress. Deciding that you will make a change, no matter what, no matter how small, that is how we get healthy. Truly healthy. I have been helping people get well for almost 30 years and I assure you, it never happens in one fell swoop. Sure, I can treat and help you feel better in the moment and often it feels like it *is* instantaneous.

To truly heal, though, to really put the body back on the right track, takes time. The amount of time is different for everyone. How long they have been sick, the patient's overall health status, their ability to comply, all those things factor in to healing time. Do they have good health habits? Are they ready to make changes?

See, true healing always requires a change. Sometimes a full-on about-face kind of change. Sometimes it's just a tweak, but it's always something new. Always. It is the changes that create the friction, the changes that take the time and potentially slow the process down. Change doesn't come easily to most people. And change is the thing that will give you the results that you want and need.

Sometimes the best way to catalyze a big change is to take the tiniest, most incremental steps. Other times it is the monumental, revolutionary changes that catapult you to the new life or the goal that you are striving for. And still other times, the step that we take might be neither. Just steps. New steps. Maybe a different movement or direction. But clearly, unless you are willing to take those steps, nothing will change.

That is the good news. There is an amazing thing that begins to happen when we learn to choose for ourselves. For me, unmet goals and dreams constantly haunt me and chase me down. For me, serving others gives me an immediate reward that easily knocks me off my path towards my own goals.

Many of us give in to our "need" for this or that in the present moment, while denying the deeper need to accomplish our goals or see a task to its completion. Many times, we mistake the surface desire for the real need, and end up missing the very thing that would keep us fulfilled. As a result, we end up chasing around things that really have no business sucking all of our time and energy.

While choosing you and your *real* needs may seem like an oversimplification, I do think this may be the real crux of the real issue. Not only that, but this is where the growth is, and ultimately the healing. I dare you to go there and go deep.

1. Take a moment and really think about what you want to accomplish.
2. What baby steps could you take right now that would get you there?
3. What epic revolutionary steps could easily catapult you toward your goal?

Day 6 - Keep moving

Life is like riding a bicycle...to stay in balance, you must stay moving. --Anonymous

This is true on so many levels. Not only do we have to stay moving to be physically healthy, our mental health is also tied directly to our ability keep moving forward. That is, working through things, changing direction when we need to, keeping ourselves fresh, not allowing stagnation. As hard as it might be to extricate ourselves from our comfort zones, it is critical that we do so.

Staying in one place, with unrealized dreams, is way more painful than stepping into my *dis*comfort zone. However, staying in motion is not as difficult as it may seem. I think we tend to overcomplicate it.

I love the idea of the next best step. We usually know what that should be. And it can often be a wonderfully easy thing. The trouble is, it is often something that we don't want to do.
It might be a hard thing or a confrontational thing or something that requires that we go out on a bit of a limb.

I personally get so wrapped up in doing the right thing that I have been known to tie myself in knots and not do anything. I have to remind myself that doing something, anything, that might take me in the direction of my dreams, will be the perfect action for today. I always feel better when I do.

Even if it only inches the needle forward or maybe not at all. In the final analysis, the process is what is important. The journey is the destination. The journey is *the* reason. The actual destination is just a bonus. This is why I love *process goals* so very much.

For example, today, you might start with walking 10 minutes, maybe tomorrow it will be 12 minutes, and then in a month, 20 minutes.

Or, in my case, today I will write one chapter, tomorrow I will edit yesterday's and write another. Before I know it, I have a book to publish. The challenge is to embrace all that goes into making each part of it happen. Even when we don't really *want* to.

Today, I encourage you to look for *your next step* and simply walk in it. Don't overcomplicate or shy away from it.

1. If you were advising a dear friend on *your* life, what would you see as the next step?
2. Are you walking with a strong cadence in the direction of your dreams?
3. If not, identify those things that are holding you back and begin to eliminate them.

You ARE worth it. I promise.

Day 7 - Wading Through the Hard

Today, I didn't want to get out of bed. Not because I was tired. Not really. That was only part of it. My shoulder and neck hurt, I had trouble sleeping, but more importantly, I didn't feel like I had anything to get up for.

Yes, I know, this is not what you want to hear in a book like this. I am supposed to have all the answers. But the truth is, I am just like you. I have good days and bad days. And mine didn't miraculously get any better, when I did eventually get up and face the day.

While I did actually get up, it was not with gratitude, nor with a very good attitude. I just showed up. I ended up getting some work done, had an argument with my husband, then talked to my sister during my lunch break. As she tried to encourage me, I yelled at her too! Here's the deal, I haven't travelled or even taken much of a break in over 2 two years.

As essential health care providers, we didn't get that break that a lot of others did in 2020. We continued to see patients and not with any more confidence that we wouldn't get sick. In other words, it *was* stressful! That probably sounds like a bit of a sob story and perhaps I am having a bit of a pity party, but I really don't mean it that way. The truth is, I don't really feel like I can quit or even want to. There is just too much work to do. And truthfully, I am okay with that.

There is powerful part of me that wants to meet with you right here on the page. More than that, a part of me longs to meet you here. There is a part of me that feels like this is home. I can let my hair down, share my hard with you and bolster you up in the process. I did pull my big girl pants on and went to work today, just like I have every other day. I waded through my *hard*, even though I thought it was impossible. And I know that if I can do it, so can you.

If you look at any job in the world, there will always be hard stuff to work through. There are challenges with getting along with people.

There are policies to be made, deadlines to be kept and things that need to be delivered.

There is always hard stuff. So, when I finally sat down to write a bit today, it felt like an elixir to my soul. It always does. And just knowing that I might help you with your *hard* makes it even better.

Here's how I will get through the rest of my day. I am going to take a few minutes to read a novel. *(Bliss!)* When I get my kids from school, I will engage deeply with whatever they have to say...my problems often fade when I put myself in the shoes of two teenagers! I will take a my sunset walk and maybe chat with a friend on the phone. I am staying moving.

Even through the sludge. I am moving through it. And closer with each step to the other side.

I will not be too busy to process and congratulate myself for what I have accomplished today. I did show up. I muscled through. And by the way, so did you.

Tomorrow will be better because we showed up and moved the needle forward today. And for that, I am thankful.

1. In what ways can you show up, even when you don't *want* to?
2. When have you shown up in the past and proved to yourself that you could?
3. How will showing up today, make tomorrow easier?

2

Discover Your Genius

Thirty years of hands-on experience as a practicing chiropractor has taught me so many wonderful lessons, but the thing that stands out above all else is this: We are fearfully and wonderfully made. Our bodies are miraculous beyond our wildest imaginings and no two of us that are exactly alike. Not only that, we are never twice the same. We are constantly growing and changing and progressing and bringing your very own brand of awesomeness into the world. Not only that, you have a particular genius that sets you apart. I promise.

You may feel like you are just average or that you are not outstanding in any way, but that, my friend, is utter hogwash. Part of the reason you feel that way is that you get to live with yourself every day! The truth is that you have so many unique giftings, that we would probably be hard-pressed to list them all. And the funny thing is, you probably take half of them for granted.

While you have met wonderful traveling companions, chances are that you only got a few moments with them, before you moved on or lost track. I think that happens for a reason. For our benefit. Maybe it is to allow us the opportunity to rise to our best. Even though we do intersect meaningfully with others, and even though we share bits and pieces of common things, we usually only get to walk together for a time, for each of us has our own journey.

If that has been your experience, I hope you realize how very special that is, and relish what you have learned together. If you get to spend months, years or a lifetime together, enjoy every minute, but don't for a minute lose yourself.

You are on this path because of a particular talent or giftedness that sets you apart. Embrace that! Learn to recognize and enjoy *your* uniqueness. Realize that God has put you right here for a reason and that it might be lonely at times..

Finally, I am convinced that the harder we work, the stronger we get. The more adversity we face, the more able we will be to face it the next time. Presuming that this is the game that we want to play, in the first place, the better off we will be, as we build these perseverance muscles and come into our own. You were made for this. Let's go.

Day 1: Calling

I have shied away from this one. Yes, there have been times in my life when I have felt so strongly the mantle of my calling, that couldn't help but recognize it and walk therein. Other times, though, I have so doubted my own qualifications or place or eligibility, that I stop my own progress before I get anywhere. I catch myself thinking: *Who am I to claim such audacity?*

Truthfully, it has become clear to me that this self-doubt is yet another veiled, albeit more complicated excuse. Yet another way of squelching our own greatness, not becoming who we were designed to be.

It seems that we tend to over-complicate this thing we deem *calling*. Why would we be here if we are an utter duplication to of the next guy? If we aren't called to something, then really, why are we here? Not everyone is called to be the President of the United States, or even the president of a local company. But every role, no matter how seemingly insignificant, can be viewed as a calling. Sometimes, viewing it this way can give us the motivation we need to stay in the game or take that role to the next level.

Each of us has been given a unique set of genetic codes, characteristics and personality traits that qualify us to do something. Or maybe more than one thing. I think it is far more offensive to our Creator, to shy away from our role out of false humility than it is to do it badly.

There is a certain merit in simply getting into the arena and trying. Trying for all we are worth. Even if we don't do it perfectly.

So, here we go. Let's start with what you love. Usually what we love comes easily and is a very natural fit. I think back to my foray into mothering. Most moms feel completely overwhelmed with the idea of doing the job of motherhood. But even with our feelings of inadequacy, there are few moms that I have met that don't *want* to. We may need to learn some things, get some practice and hone our skills, but the *want to* tells us the truth about calling.

While our natural giftedness can set us up for ease, our calling is not necessarily easy. This is a hard one to swallow. Although we may have talents in a certain area, finding and fulfilling our calling may be the hardest, trickiest, most elusive thing that we ever do. But let's not mistake hard for wrong.

The Bible says that *"in this world, you will have many troubles, but take heart, I have overcome the world..."* **John 16:33**

I think that speaks to being in the right place at the right time, and having problems still.

One of the best things we can do for the next generation is *model the process* of both finding and fulfilling our personal calling...How else will they understand how to find theirs?" By following hard after our own path, we give others license to follow theirs. And taking it a step further, what is to be gained really, by shying away or shrinking from your own greatness or making yourself small?

"Our deepest fear is not that we are inadequate. Our deepest fear is that we are powerful beyond measure. It is our light, not our darkness that most frightens us. We ask ourselves, 'Who am I to be brilliant, gorgeous, talented, fabulous?'

Actually, who are you not to be? You are a child of God. Your playing small does not serve the world. There is nothing enlightened about shrinking so that other people won't feel insecure around you. We are all meant to shine, as children do. We were born to make manifest the glory of God that is within us. It's not just in some of us; it's in everyone. And as we let our own light shine, we unconsciously give other people permission to do the same. As we are liberated from our own fear, our presence automatically liberates others."

---- Marianne Williamson, <u>A Course in Miracles</u>

1. Who are you liberating with your willingness to shine?

2. Do you catch yourself shying away from your calling? Why or why not?
3. What can you do today that moves you back towards your purpose?

Day 2: Because Yours is a Unique Contribution

No two of us that are exactly alike. In our typical day-to-day interactions, with family members, co-workers and even best friends, we are often reminded that we don't always see eye-to-eye. Over the past week, I have been emailing and calling my sister with regards to an upcoming gathering, and I was reminded just how different we are.

We share the same parents, both mother and father; she is my blood, we were raised in the same house. Yet, her views of the world and the way she makes decisions couldn't be more different than my own. I can see that her way of viewing the world suits her life very well. I admire her resolve and how she upholds her own needs and personal values.

My world is very different and yet, when we come together, we share an undeniable link: our childhood, our heritage. As I was laughing about our differences last week, I couldn't help but take away this practical application. If siblings can be this different, then most assuredly, we have been gifted in very distinct ways for a very important reason. Absolutely *no one*, shares your exact vision, experience, and unique perspective on things. It really is *up to each of us* to bring our distinctiveness to the table.

And to the table did we come. I think fondly of the many decadent meals I enjoyed. Family gatherings were eating extravaganzas! Our family of origin knew the value of eating well and working it off. I have an aunt, who can still bake an angel food cake that is so melt-in-your-mouth-amazing that you are sure from the very first bite that you are eating a little bit of heaven.

It never really registered until much later, when I was no longer attending these family gatherings, that the meal depended on each family bringing their best to the table. Literally homespun and from scratch. Homemade or don't bother.

I find that I often disqualify myself, by my own misguided self-talk, thinking somehow, that if I don't have it all figured out, that I will have *nothing* to offer. As I think back over those amazing meals, always way too much food, always something new to try, and always so much amazing variety, I have to wonder what would have happened if everyone thought they weren't good enough to contribute.

These reunions would easily top fifty people without much effort, so for one, it wouldn't take long to run out of food...an outrage in a family that prides itself above all else to be well-fed.

The other thing that this taught me was to just bring it. *Just bring it.* My mom would be known to lug a salad, a side dish, and a lasagna for good measure. Not to mention a dessert or two and any surplus from her garden.

When I think about her surpluses, I see God's amazing economy. My mom would always bring what she had. She is the most generous person I know. She navigated the tumultuous waters of raising two teenaged daughters, single-handedly, widowed young, and I believe that God blessed her by filling her cup to overflowing. She never stopped bringing and giving, even when she was scraping the bottom of her own barrel. As a result, we have never gone hungry.

Bring what you have. It is yours to hoard, or hide under a bushel. Today, before you quit, I encourage you to think about your life as a banquet, not for the taking or consumption, but a banquet that we get to help put on. Then think about what the banquet could be, if you shared from your *very best* and allowed someone to be nourished by it.

It really is that simple. Do what you do, bring it to the best of your ability, and let those around you enjoy your unique flavor. This is what makes life interesting and the thing that will most surely bless you beyond your wildest imagination.

1. What do *you* have to bring? That is, what is your very own secret sauce or superpower?
2. When and where can you bring it?
3. What is holding you back from doing so?

Day 3 - Trust Your Intuition

Intuition has always fascinated me. How is it that we just know things? That gut feeling, the feeling that something just doesn't feel right. And then discovering after the fact, that you are 100% right.

When we trust it, intuition can be our best friend. When we ignore it, though, I think it ignores us back. Or could it be, that if we ignore it long enough, we become functionally deaf? Frustrated by your ignore-ance, maybe intuition will find someone else who is willing pay attention. Perhaps it moves on to someone who is willing to hear it out, implement its ideas, go to work on its behalf. Somewhere warmer, more stable, more favorable.

Intuition is that still small voice that is the accumulation of all our acquired wisdom, previous education, and experience. As part of the unconscious, and unlike our finite minds, intuition has the ability to sift through the entirety of all that has gone before. An amazing feat, but this is not the only reason we should listen. Having been with you since the beginning, your intuition also knows you. It has the ability to reflect your deepest desires and how to handle everything in this context. It knows how to guide you, if given half a chance.

So, if we are going to trust it, how do we know if it is, in fact, trustworthy? Think about what you are listening to, tuning into, hanging out with, aspiring to. All of that will store in that precious brain of yours. In addition to expressing the totality of who you are, your intuition will be the eventual product of what you feed it.

If you feed your mind and heart with life-giving material, like faith, hope, and inspiration, your intuition will likely be worthy of your unwavering trust. If, on the other hand, you allow your mind to be filled with thoughts that like fear and doubt, the result will be an intuition that feeds you ideas and suggestions that reflect exactly that.

So, I challenge you today, to feed your mind well. Fill your mind with thoughts of positivity, hope, love...all the good stuff. Then learn how to listen and trust it, knowing that your own intuition wants only the best for you.

Listen carefully, move forward, and don't stop. Your very life depends on it.

1. Has your intuition been whispering to you lately?
2. Grab a notebook, listen carefully and start writing.
3. If it hasn't, make a point of stopping to listen, today. You might be surprised by what you hear...

Day 4 - Yes, Right Now! Before You Get Derailed

Have you ever had this experience? You set a specific goal, complete with a massive to-do list. You picture yourself doing the work and achieving the goal. You can almost taste the victory. And then, as the busyness of the day overtakes you, you decide, even while fully conscious, to completely ignore all of it.

We will eat better tomorrow when that cake is gone, when the kids are back in school, or when we can get home in time to cook. Excuses rage on and on, as we allow ourselves to become oblivious to any goal we might have set today, yesterday, last week, or last month.

Here's an example: Our family ate out last night. Unfortunately the splurge was not even remotely close to Five-Star cuisine and definitely not worth the extra pound that I gained on top of the one I gained the day before. Yes, I gained 2 two pounds in as many days, when my long-term goal has been to lose five. It seems there was no good reason for the eating out, either. No birthday, we weren't on the road, no practices, just a vague desire not to cook. Sound familiar?

We have to eat to survive, so we can't give up food completely. We have to learn how to moderate. There is always a way to rationalize or cheat or put one more bite in our salivating mouths. Trouble is, that small bite is enough to change our body chemistry and trigger a whole cascade of chemical changes that make us want to eat more of that bad thing.

So it is goes with our life's work. We have to do something, right? It is so easy to just go with the flow and do the next thing that comes down the pike, rather than be purposeful about what your next best thing could be. It is so easy to get sucked into all those default roles, while the things that we really want to be doing, get pushed aside.

Hence the title for today: *Yes! Right Now*...That's before someone else's project finds you. Before you forget how much you love it. Maybe your distractions are noble, things like helping kids with their homework, working on one of your husband's pet projects, saying yes to a little bit of overtime at work. I have been there and done all of it and there is a time and place for this. However, when all of that stuff consistently supersedes your own passion projects, that's where you may have to draw the line.

My writing often gets pushed to the back burner when things get busy around my house or at the clinic. Rather than making the writing a daily discipline, I have allowed it to take second place to so many other things.

The net result, over time, is that I have moments of full-on resentment for all I am doing for everyone else. In reality, none of my people have any idea of the sacrifice I am making for them!

When I get more consistent with my discipline of honoring my writing time, I realize how much joy my writing brings to my life. And how much saner I am. I am infinitely more able to get all the rest of it done, and done with a joy and efficiency that cannot coexist with that latent resentment.

Don't to try to do ten things. Focus on *one thing* and see where that might lead. Remember, we are trying to focus on your genius. Perhaps today you need to set aside time with your spouse, or your kids. Maybe it is time to make that call, apply for that job, sit down, and begin *your* writing. In other words, make your own "calling" your priority.

Today, I encourage you to choose your own work. Choose for you and do what you were called to do. Fiercely fight off all the dragons of distraction, armed with your very own list of exactly what you want to get done today. Make your work and your days your own. I dare you to start today.

Only you can choose you. I promise you that you will end the day feeling great about what you have accomplished. Chances are, all those other tasks for all your people will somehow get done, too.

Trust the process. And yes, do it now.

1. Set a goal, make your to do list, put it on your calendar, and do it.

2. Yes, it is as important as everyone's else list! Write your stuff on there too!
3. If that doesn't work today, change your course, shift things around, but keep heading towards your goal...even if it is just a little bit each day.

Day 5 - Not Looking Forward to it Today

It is Friday and this week has been intense. I am tired. My leg is aching, my other hip hurts, and I am feeling totally inadequate to meet the demands of this day.

I messed up on Wednesday, forgetting (or maybe not tuning into?) the practice schedule, and I was late to pick up my kids from practice. We were crazy at the clinic and a short stop there to check on a few things, got to be a long one, as I got wrapped up in the work.

When I glanced at my phone, there were multiple messages telling me to **come now,** practice had been over for 20 minutes. I was happily seeing patients while the coaches waited on me to fetch my children! Horrified by my oversight, I apologized to everyone I could. But the truth was, I was ashamed.

Why does it something like this bother me so much? Well, first, I have been conditioned to never, ever let anyone down. I am supposed to be on the giving end always, never taking or asking anyone for favors. Clearly, this is some messed up thinking, and I probably need to let it go.

Secondly, I really did plan ahead. I really was very well-intended, I did everything right with my planning. Unfortunately, I forgot to look at the actual schedule as I was executing. I made a simple mistake.

Thankfully, God is not too busy to notice my oversight and He had this all in His hands. He had everything and everybody covered, and the truth is, they really needed me at the office that day. Perhaps, God allowed me to forget the schedule so that I could have the extra 20 minutes of time for seeing patients? It sure seemed that way.

I am indulging myself and allowing myself to feel daunted by the busy day I have scheduled today. Because I made a simple mistake two days ago, I am doubting my ability to keep up with it. Will I mess up again? Do we have enough resources to cover the demands of the day?

This is a perfect moment to take a look at how our brains tend to sabotage us. And the perfect time to check in with our genius. While I need to be careful that I don't over-schedule, at the same time, I can't lose all trust in my ability to do hard things.

Instead, I am choosing thoughts that will serve me today. The truth is, that I am very good at juggling it all most of the time, and I will be fine with the schedule, as long as I remember to look at it. Having learned from my mistake, I will look closely at the pickup time today. I am a great planner, and an even better one now.

1. What mistakes have made you hesitant to move forward boldly today? Is it worth the hesitation?
2. How have those mistakes made you who you are today?
3. Moving forward and taking all of that with you, how can you make today great?

Day 6 - What is Your Genius?

Now, before you argue that you don't have any genius or that if you do, you sure don't know what it is, let me remind you that you are, in fact, made in the very image of God! You have a beautiful array of skills and talents that no one else on the planet possesses, whether you want to admit it or not. Skills and talents that set you apart, that literally make you...you.

It is those things that I really want you to take some time, right now, to think about. It is those things that we are going to spend some time honoring and cultivating. This is all about you. Not what you think you should be doing, based on your vocation, or your finances, or what someone else thinks you are good at.

We are going to hone in on what you want, believe in, and are *most* passionate about. Gay Hendricks in The Big Leap: Conquer Your Hidden Fear & Take Life to the Next Level explains how many of us spend our lives in the *Zone of Excellence.* Much to the chagrin and outright neglect of our actual genius. If this was a benign mistake with little consequence, it might be fine to do this. Many of us spend a lifetime here. The trouble is, you were actually made to do *your* genius thing. And the longer you spend in your *Zone of Excellence,* the harder it becomes to shift into your *Zone of Genius.*

Here is the good news. If you are ignoring your genius, the thing that lights you up, it will likely not let you go. There will be a constant niggling. A constant frustration. A constant feeling of incongruence that will not leave you alone. And if you should finally begin to listen, this may be when your life will get really exciting.

You wonder why I speak with such conviction? Because I have personally been there. And yes, I have had frustrations and outright failures as a result. Here's the deal. You can get away with this. Not living in your genius. People around you who enjoy the benefits of your excellence would love for you to stay right where you are. However, if you continue to move along this path, there will be no one to fulfill *your* actual calling. That thing that only you can do. And yes, this is a very big deal.

Today, I want you to assess your congruence, your personal alignment with your own truth. If you were to die tomorrow, could you honestly say you invested most of your time in something that really lit you up? I know it sounds a bit strong, but this is a great way to determine if we are really on track. So be brutally honest with yourself. Then get ready to dive into your divine calling.

Get ready to have the time of your life.

1. How many times this week did you feel like you were answering your true calling?
2. How many times this week did you feel that you were spending an inordinate amount of time fostering someone else's dream?
3. What small shift can you make today to get you doing what you really want to do, each day?

Day 7 - Are You Doing Exactly What You *Want* to Do?

So, what you actually *want* to do offers some really clear clues as to what you your life's work might be. It is interesting to me how many people do something that is very different than what they really, truly want to do.

We go to work at jobs that have little or nothing to do with the passion projects that fill our evenings, our weekends, or our imaginations. We go to work, for the majority of our week, seemingly to fund the thing that actually lights us up. Then we pack as much of our passion projects into our time off that we can afford. Often exhausting ourselves, neglecting important things and feeling frustrated all the while. We end up, in effect, living our lives in reverse.

Or even worse, we spend our lives, literally spending all our energy, doing something that has little or nothing to do with our passions. So we end up numb to the guilt, the shame or the raw pain of denying who we really are.

I have personally lived the principle of "work before play", denying myself with a finely tuned ability to delay gratification. It has served me well, allowing me to achieve consistent success professionally for many years. Since I love to write, I have always struggled to allow myself the indulgence in the luxury of writing. It is too much like play. Simply too enjoyable to be counted as work.

How this plays out in real life is that my real work is never really done. And, if the work is never done...I can never write. This hasn't gone on for weeks or months, which might be understandable. This has stopped me for years. Years of literally putting off what I *want* to do, so that I could get done what I had to do.

I have not only lost out on the pure enjoyment of writing and creating, I have caught myself becoming resentful for all that I have lost. I resent the work, the people, all the stuff that took me away from the writing.

Sure, I was able to function in the face of it and even do things that I really didn't want to do. The trouble is, all of the self-denial did not bode well for my happiness. I am sure that it showed up, not only in my effectiveness, but in my performance. It is so not worth it.

This book was written as I walked the hard road of coming back to myself. The hard road of reconciling my own differences with myself. The hard road of denying myself the easy road of busyness, in exchange for the heart-driven work that I truly longed to do.

I hope that as we walk through these chapters together, that you will fan into flame that little spark that that God has planted in you. That little spark that not only defines who you are, but *whose* you are. That little spark that can easily get snuffed out in the busyness of your days. It is that spark that is the essence of who you are and what you are called to do.

I pray that as you pursue your Creator and all He has for you, your creative spark will become an inextinguishable fire. One that will burn brightly with the light of your unique truth. Trust me when I say that it is absolutely worth the hard work of living out your dreams. Trust me when I say that you will enjoy the journey and the hard road back.

Honestly, what I have found to be true, is that it doesn't feel like work when I am fully aligned with my very own true north. Sometimes, it means working harder than I have ever worked before, but the work is nurturing, soul-quenching, and even rejuvenating! This is the way it should be.

It is time to rise above all the reasons why it won't work and begin to believe in the possibilities of your dreams. God placed them in your heart for a reason. Once we have identified what we should be doing, it is our job find a compelling why.

For me, I sometimes have to remind myself that I am doing the creative work of writing - just because I want to. And that is reason enough. But, further, I know that if God has gifted me with a message, I need to share what I am learning and discovering.

I am confident that you were made with a love of something, or a gifting for a reason. That particular strength or interest sets you apart. He wants to use you in the thing that you love above all else. This is why, even though you may accomplish amazing things *outside* of your gifting, it always feels like a bit of a hollow victory. This is why you feel like you are always searching for the life you really want.

You are not alone. Today, I encourage you to embrace your *genius* and do more of that...just because. It is time.

1. If you could do anything in the world, paid or unpaid, what would it be?
2. If money were no object, what would you do with your time?
3. How have you seen that your particular gifting effortlessly touches the world?

3

Avoiding Pain

People go to the greatest of lengths to avoid pain. We stop moving, we take over-the-counter and prescription pain meds. We eat or drink or shop, abuse substances or micro-manage...all with the goal to eliminate pain, discomfort or any other unpredictable emotion. , we mask it through eating or drinking or shopping or substance abuse or micro-managing...at eliminating pain, discomfort, or any other unpredictable emotion.

Your motto might be to avoid pain at all costs. Rather than deal with another moment of discomfort, we stay ultra-busy, we don't feel. We move on, we don't process. Or perhaps like me, you do process, then berate yourself or over-analyze to a point where you can't get up off the couch. No chance to try for anything.

If this is you, I want you to know that it doesn't have to be this way. Whether we are talking about your work, your passion project, or your relationships, you actually can begin to set goals again and you can enjoy the journey. Over the short haul, I suppose, eliminating pain could be beneficial. Sometimes the body legitimately needs a break, a rest. Time to heal, time to take things down a notch, to repair. Long term, though, taking it easy can make our physical body weaker, less tolerant of activity, work, and stress, and ultimately *sicker*. While it may *feel* better in the moment to take it easy on ourselves, this is clearly not a permanent solution.

Avoiding work pain, for instance, will probably lead to more negative consequences, most of which, will probably not serve you well. You avoid it long enough and you will develop a cascade of problems and of course, avoiding *those* problems will lead to more of them. While control can look very appealing on the outside, it can be a devastating shackle. Keep at it long enough and your bondage grows. The irony is that control is an illusion.

We simply cannot master our environment with control. The efforts to do so can be boring, unrewarding, and decidedly not fun. Over-rated. So, why and how do we fall into this trap? This is exactly what we will delve into this week. Let's take a close look at how we might be *Avoiding Pain* and what we can do about it.

Day 1: Trusting vs. Avoidance

We had a staff member quit yesterday. It feels a bit like a sucker punch. I really like her and was shocked when she simply walked out. She was done. Truthfully, though, she had quit a long time ago. This was just the physical manifestation of it. It made me realize again, that I don't want to.

Quit, that is. Go, if you may, but I'm not. I'm here, still trying, still working, contributing, because it it is the right thing to do. And I will keep doing it. It feels really good to declare my territory out loud, stake my claim on not quitting, stand firm in my commitment to keep going on my journey, the journey that some may readily give up on.

Last week, when she was a bit disgruntled and the thought of losing her was just a notion, I was scared of it. I didn't want to lose her. I really wanted it all to work out. But then again, we simply couldn't go on doing what we were doing, or in this case, *not* doing. She was not really doing her job, not really present. Put simply, she had already quit. And I didn't have the courage to face it, I didn't have the courage to end our relationship, I didn't have the courage to push her beyond her limits and our bottom line was suffering as a result. I admit, it was because I like her too much. I didn't want to lose the relationship.

So, what did I learn? Several things. I re-learned the importance of taking action and believing in myself, in my own judgment, my ability to accurately assess situations, and move accordingly.

I was reminded that I am held. I was reminded that God is always in it, with me, no matter what. I learned that I need to make the decision and be willing to pivot quickly, not for me, but for the business, for the rest of the staff, and even the patients. They are all counting on me.

It boils down to trust, really. Trusting myself and God and the process of things. Trusting that letting go is sometimes the better way. Trusting that holding a staff member to their commitments is always the right thing, even if *they* don't agree. Trusting that I don't always have all the answers, but that *He* does.

Trust in the Lord with all your heart and lean not on your own understanding. In all your ways acknowledge Him and He will direct your path. ---Proverbs 3:5,6

1. He truly has my back and will never quit on me.
2. In what way can you trust your intuition more fully today?
3. Is there a decision/change that you need to make that you are shying away from?
4. Take that step of faith today and then journal how you felt and what you learned. Trust that you will be held...

Day 2: But it's Just Too Hard!

I am exhausted. Completely and utterly. My real job is sucking the life out of me. I can't seem to get any momentum going on any front. I am talking about survival-type things. Things like eating well, exercising, enjoying friends and family and, of course, my writing. It is seems to take too much energy, so I fritter away what little time I have. I am easily distracted by Facebook, work drama or Amazon shopping. I'd much rather stroll the online aisles, amidst the after-Christmas sales. What if I miss out on something?

I suspect that I am not alone in this. It is always easier to consume than produce. So, why is it that we can't seem to get to it and actually do something? In my case, I know there is at least a small part of me that doesn't actually want to finish the manuscript, because then I will have to begin the hard work of finding someone to like the work and buy it! I have been through the long journey to publication.

So, here I am in the midst of it all. I acknowledge that it is, indeed, very hard. There is nothing easy about the discipline, the forsaking of the novel that I am reading for enjoyment, the setting aside of the time, from friends or family. Even as I write today, my son is begging me to play with him and although I really want to, I also really want to do this. I really want to make some progress. I really want to accomplish something. I have been programmed to put work ahead of play, and so, it is almost impossible for me to enjoy play when I haven't done some real work first.

Plus, I think I ate too much for lunch. I am sluggish, lethargic, and bloated. I am just not in the playing mood. Am I in the writing mood? Not really. In between his pleads for attention, I catch myself nodding off, my eyes fully closed, my fingers moving over the keyboard in a sort of meditative sleep-writing.

And yet, this shows me that I have come up with another reason to not quit. Somehow the doing of this work, brings a certain satisfaction that I long for. Whether I will ever have the luxury of publication or not, it is enough that I am doing this, right now.

So today, whatever it is that makes your heart sing, do it with gusto. For this is the stuff of life. This very well could be the thing that you are here to do. It seems that more often than not, we have to fight for the right to actually do it. We have jobs, housekeeping, families to feed, and recreation.

Jonnie finally decided that he didn't want to wait me out and went to badger his sister to play. I am relieved, and a bit saddened, and so I trudge on. This "hard" is one of the reasons I know I must do this work with you, because it is probably hard for you too. I am struggling right alongside you. Every bit of work is eked out and forced to the page defying all the wily forces that are battling against me.

Ironically, today, the words seem to come so easily when I let the ideas flow and I let the process take over. Eyes fully closed now, I pray for the strength to continue. I pray for the wisdom to encourage you with the deepest sincerity. Not giving up for a minute, but instead, carrying this thing through to the very end. Yes, even *the hard*.

1. What feels just too hard for you right now?
2. Could it be that digging in and doing it might be the very best thing for you?
3. What if taking small steps makes it way easier than you think?
4. What small steps can you take today?

Day 3: Because it is Supposed to be Hard

"Anything worth doing is worth doing well..." I have lived by this. I think we can take it a step further with "Anything worth doing well is supposed to be hard".

Tom Hanks said, "If it was easy, everyone would be doing it."

Every time I sit down at my computer, I realize how hard this is. To fit everything in around this. To distill all the big concepts in my brain into useable, practical things that might actually help us all move forward. To figure out the essentials, make it worth your while, too.

It is unbelievably hard, especially knowing that there is a chance that no one will read it. There is an equal chance that it will get read, but not understood. That it will fall flat. But, alas, I must remind myself why I am pursuing this. I write because it it is right. I write because it is my right. I write because if I don't, I'm not quite right.

Maybe today I needed this reminder that I write because it is not easy. There is something in me that loves the challenge and maybe any potential glory. And to agree with Mr. Hanks, "If it were easy, everyone would be doing it."

The result is to put things right, even if it is only for me. And perhaps by doing that, the world is a slightly better place. I am confident as I push through the hard parts, it will be just a bit easier tomorrow.

So, today, I encourage you to do your hard thing, whatever that may be. Do it with gusto, because it is supposed to be hard. You are my hero for doing it. I can almost feel your energy as I write these words. I promise that you are building hard muscles that will make it easier to do it next time.

1. What is your hard thing?
2. Why do you do it? Or avoid it?
3. How is it getting easier?

4. Journal how you might use that momentum to move yourself forward.

Day 4: Procrastination 101

I have noticed that it is very hard to improve at my skills when I am doing nothing. Sure, a case can be made for pre-planning for success. However, we have to actually move forward in order to make progress. Once again, this might seem oversimplified, but for someone like me: super-analytical, hyper-focused, I can easily talk myself out of any action, by over-focussing on the planning.

If you are like me, we need to stop beating ourselves up and just do the work. It seems universally human to procrastinate. Of course, some of us are better than others at beating this demon. Somehow, I know that I if I am struggling with this and you aren't yet, you are just putting it off...your time will come!

It seems that procrastination is part of the human condition, the ultimate pain-avoidance technique.

Trouble is, in most things, if we avoid doing what needs to be done, our situation can't possibly improve. And while we might avoid the acute pain in the moment, we will be forced to face the potentially deeper pain of unmet goals and dreams. Far deeper and far more reaching pain, I am sure.

I want to remind you, that being weak or bad at something is no reason to stop. With every word I write, I trust that I am getting better. With every song you sing, you will become a better singer. Doing nothing allows us to get better at well...at exactly nothing. I know this is harsh, but unfortunately true.

My husband has been known to say, "Do something, even if it is wrong." He is above all things, a man of action. Although admittedly, every single thing he does may not be the exact right thing in that moment, he catches the right thing more often than not, simply because he is in motion. I so admire that quality in him. And I know that I am not the only one who does. He has earned the rightful position of being the *go-to* guy in almost every circle he inhabits.

While he may not know the exact next step, he is never afraid to try something, anything, to keep the train moving forward.

So, today I am writing because I know that I will get better. I know that this will be a better manuscript simply for having worked at it. And there may be a little less procrastination in the world because I am encouraging you to give it up, one step at a time.

That, to me, is worth the time and effort. Less quitting means more productive doing, which leads to more happiness. Ultimately to this broken world being a better place.

1. Think about the last time you overcame your own procrastination. What were you able to do or accomplish?
2. Are you avoiding your best life's work by putting it off in some way?
3. Instead of beating yourself up for what you are not doing, I dare you to pour all your energy into getting stuff done. What is one thing that you can do today?

Day 5 - There Will *Never* be a Perfect Time

I really tried to plan our first pregnancy. Having watched from the sidelines, I studied the calendar, not wanting to be fully pregnant in the heat of the summer, or the dead of winter. I wondered if we could time everything so that the baby would be fully ready at exactly the right time. I was trying to plan for the baby to fit neatly into my already overly hectic schedule. I was not only trying to control every aspect of this thing that I knew nothing about, but I was trying to make perfect decisions ahead of time.

We waited on purpose, so I was a bit older than the average mom. We were going to do it right! As anyone will tell you, there is no perfect time or way to have children. In fact, kids really do tend to make a bit of a mess of the perfectly organized order of our lives. However, as we respond to their needs or meet them in whatever crisis, it brings out the very best in us. We learn how to re-order perfectly on the fly, in the moment.

Likewise, as we force ourselves to do that thing, right now, that might feel inopportune or even out of order, that thing that has us stressed to the max, that thing that has us confused or daunted or paralyzed, it is in that process that we will become our very best selves. In our response, as we rise to the meeting of the need, we are forced to call upon resources from the deepest parts of ourselves. We all tend to do this extremely well, when we have to.

We are actually made to do this. We are made to rise to the occasion in the moment. Made to do our best work when we have to, in the crunch. Even better, though, when we acknowledge our inadequacies and fully surrender, calling upon God to show up in us and for us. This is when miracles happen. It is only through the fire that we realize we actually have the abilities we need to handle the tough stuff.

So, today, instead of waiting for the perfect time, go ahead and just do it. Do something!

There will never be a perfect time. To think so is foolish. A waste of precious time and precious energy. In fact, it could be argued that the longer we wait, the harder it is to get down to this business of getting it done. Why make it harder?

Getting back to our family. When we finally made the decision to try for that first baby, it took several years longer than we could have ever guessed. By the time we finally conceived, we were no longer looking at how the pregnancy would land on the calendar. We were just thrilled to have a baby on the way.

In the end, though, our kids were born to parents who could not have been more excited...and both of them in the heat of summer! It all could not have been more perfect and almost none of it happened the way I had planned.

1. Have you been waiting, over-analyzing, or biding your time to begin or re-engage in your passion project?
2. What is holding you back? Make a list of all these things.
3. Now, one-by-one, blast through your excuses and get it done. There couldn't be a better time.

Day 6 - What's the One Thing That Makes You Uncomfortable?

Getting out of your comfort zone is where the pay-dirt is. It doesn't matter what your goals, your vocation, or whether you are trying to learn a new skill, there will inevitably be uncomfortable things along the way. Things that you don't know about ahead of time, that might confuse you or throw you for an unexpected loop. There is upside, though. It is that same discomfort that will force you to grow and develop and expand.

Further, any big change that we face can be super-uncomfortable. While we know that this it is a fact of life, that nothing stays the same forever, forcing change or even reacting to it is rarely an easy thing.

Today, as I sat down to write, I was a bit overwhelmed with this idea. Writing can be uncomfortable at times. It forces me to look at the essence of my life. It forces me to look at what I am doing that might need to be changed or tweaked, so that I am not a hypocrite with the very things that I am writing about.

When I share what I think are nuggets of truth, I want to be sure that the nuggets will be of true value for you and not just lofty platitudes that look good or have a nice ring to them. I hope and pray that you learn something, apply new things and take valuable strides in the direction of your dreams.

This is one of the many ways that "iron sharpens iron". This is just one of the ways that we learn and become better with the help of our community. As I persist and step out of my comfort zone, I hope to inspire and bring insight to you.

So today, I want you to risk being uncomfortable in your truth. Face your truth, whatever it may be, and make a decision to move forward. Do that one thing that will expand or change or grow your little world. Then watch for the miracles and the ripple-effects.

Picture for a moment a beautiful body of water, a secluded lake on a sun-drenched day. It is pristine, tranquil, reflecting a perfect sky...until something penetrates the perfect mirror of the surface. As the sun now touches the ripples, they sparkle, dance, and glimmer in a way that makes the lake even more beautiful. It is not perfectly calm anymore, but definitely more interesting!

So it is with your life. Allow something uncomfortable to invade your surface. Have the courage to allow something new to stir up your calm. The ripple effects will be dazzling.

1. I dare you to be dazzling. You got this!
2. Identify the uncomfortable change that you know could enhance or make your life better.
3. Take one small step towards making the change.
4. Set some big goals around the change. Get ready for the ripples!

Day 7 - Even When No One Else Around You is Working!

I struggle with this. Perhaps it is all the years of hearing almost as a mantra: "Hard work is akin to godliness". Or more accurately, there is no godliness without hard work. It was never optional for me.
I can easily cajole myself into staying late at the office, doing one more load of laundry, or picking up just a few things on a quick grocery run. And of course, even easier for me when everyone else is doing it with me.

One of the hardest things for me to handle is the solitary nature of the writing craft. Some days, it is all I can do seclude myself. I secretly hope that someone, anyone, will happen by and ask for favor, something productive to be done...like getting them a snack or finding their favorite pair of socks. Something "important" like that.

I am embarrassed to admit that I almost dive at those opportunities. Maybe it is to prove my worth, my value? I know, this sounds ridiculous, even to me. Part of it is the loneliness of being here, completely on my own and knowing it is all up to me. There is a part of me that gets validation from doing things for someone else. Meeting someone else's needs, even if it means ignoring my own.

With a project like this, there really is no intrinsic validation. It is a long road to publication and longer still before anyone reads the work. However, if I am honest with myself, that is not the thing that is keeping me going anyway. So, why is it that I go after outward validation, charging after it, like a fish to water, like a starving man to food?

I think it is a matter of getting to your most meaningful, motivating validation. We need to determine that sometimes our most important work will get no visible, external acknowledgement. The most important work we do is for ourselves. I have learned to stop myself from thinking that is selfish.

At times, I am so convinced, that it seems I am actually avoiding this work. The *urgent* needs of my family will easily supersede my personal needs or goals. It seems this is wired into our very DNA as women.

But, alas, to my credit, the very fact the I am doing this, right now, with no one to answer to, is its own validation. The fact that it continually and successfully pulls me back in, tells me that there is something to it. And so it is for you.

The next time you find yourself resisting because there is something that is seemingly more urgent than your passion project, try this: Pat yourself on the back, give yourself a round of applause for your due-diligence, then...get to work.

That resistance might be the most convincing evidence that you are exactly where you need to be.

1. Can you see a pattern with the things that distract you?
2. Make a list of all those things and slot them into your schedule. Before you add them in, be sure that they are all really necessary and not simply distractions.
3. Now, get to work...and don't forget to have some fun.

DR. LAURA SPARKS

4

Relishing Pleasure

Most of what we do falls into one of two categories: To avoid pain or produce pleasure. You can look back over your life and probably see a pretty clear pattern. You have likely majored in one or the other.

In the last chapter we addressed avoiding pain, now we will look at relishing pleasure. Maybe like me, you are more motivated to seek pleasure than to avoid pain. Perhaps for you, the motivation to do something that produces obvious fun or joy is more motivating than avoiding the pain associated with doing it wrong. Maybe you feel like me, that doing anything is better than doing nothing.

If that is the case, you may often find yourself exhausted by the efforts you are making to stay in the game. Efforts that are sometimes futile, sometimes make you feel like a failure, and often leave you feeling drained.

This section is all about how healthy pleasure can help you to stay in your game. How pursuing pleasure can often help you stay motivated, giving you joy, and fuel to your purpose.

Welcome to the fun.

Day 1: For the Love...

In her amazing book <u>For the Love: Fighting for Grace in a World of Impossible Standards,</u> Jen Hatmaker, talks about faith and life and how to live for the love of it without a bit of shrinking back. Her writing is fun, poignant, and spot-on.

It occurred to me that this is as great a reason as any to not quit. In other words, we stay in the game for the love. We keep going because we have chosen this life or path or project for the very love of that thing.

Sometimes that *love* gets buried amongst all the nonsense that we have to face just to do our jobs. Should we give in to the naysayers or be swayed by those that might choose to do the very same thing in a different way or for a different reason?

Today I am writing because I love it. For the very love and no other reason. I love stringing words together like a beautiful tapestry, with the hope that my heart will touch yours for even the briefest moment. Sometimes, I *like* who I am when I am doing this. I notice that I can take in my world with more honesty and clarity, when I have been forced to distill my thoughts to their barest bones. To their essence. I *like* who I am when I have had the opportunity to meet that deep need within me to get these thoughts out of my head, rather than allowing them to ricochet endlessly in my tired brain. Frankly, my mind gets tired of the echoes, the lack of resolution.

Elizabeth Gilbert, in Big Magic, talks about the danger of writing for the benefit or healing or even the assumed "fixing" of your audience. "Please don't, because your writing will most surely suffer for it," she offers. I think that is good advice.

While I would love someone to get *something* out of this, I can see that it could smack of bossiness or be simply be too heavy-handed in the fixing. I don't love being told what to do. And, I am guessing, neither do you. That is not my intent with this book and so I strongly *encourage* you to do your thing, your job, your creativity...*for the love.* This should be squarely in the realm of "for *your* sake", "for *your* health" and "for *your* benefit".

Surely, there is something that you *love* to do. So go do it, relax, and enjoy the journey.

1. Find out what you love to do...and do it with all your might.
2. What do you want to do today *for the love?*
3. Can you see how that thing might contribute to someone else's happiness?
4. How does doing that thing make you a better person?

Day 2: Identity

What makes you smile? What makes you cry? What makes you sing, dance, hug someone? If you could do anything you wanted, regardless of being paid, what would it be?

We spend so much time taking care of the mundane, the running of things, the arranging of people, and activities, that we often forget the things that are most essential. To our well-being. To our mental health. Or at least I do. The things that nurture us.

Even as I write this, I am thinking, distracted about what I am making for dinner, which isn't actually due for another five hours. Why? Because between now and then, I have countless things that need to be attended to: work, kids, putting out fires. I need to put in a bit of thought or planning time to be ready.

Even as I scold myself for being distracted, I realized that feeding my family is part of my essence. I love producing delicious, nutritious meals and then seeing my family thrive as a result. It seems that I often sacrifice my pleasure for their health and well-being. It is no contest, really. It doesn't even really feel like a sacrifice.

Are there times when grabbing a meal "out", might unload me a bit and give me the margin I need to keep writing? Sure. And so, for now, I will ignore the niggling guilt that I should be planning that today's meal. And keep writing.

The pleasure of putting words to the page in the moment, far outweighs my need to assuage my own guilt with doing the responsible thing and eating in."But we have all these groceries!" I argue in my mind. And to that, I reply, "Yes, and tomorrow we will eat that."

Admittedly, my husband and kids enjoy the break from mom's cooking as much as I enjoy the break from the labor. I need not stress over this. Even so, there is something in me that isn't quite comfortable with my breaking from the norm, the mundane. Is this really *who I am*? Do I need to cook *every* meal to be fully me?

Another big part of who I am, my essence, is my running, my working out and the ability to be consistent with moving my body, no matter what. Staying in *that* game has somehow been very easy for me. It is a non-negotiable. It is rare that more than two days in a row go by without a run, workout, yoga session, or at least something to re-connect me to my physical body.

People often ask me how I do it. I can honestly say, it is because I know who I am. I relish, and enjoy the time, even though the work can be painful, difficult. My runs often feel like a kind of coming home. As I get back into my body, out of my head, out of everyone else's business, I am rejuvenated, refreshed, renewed, *reminded* of my identity. I am a runner, who does not give up...for the love.

Today, I am granting myself the luxury of writing time. Because I am also a writer. A few precious moments of play, can easily morph into an hour. I savor the time even as it flies by, again feeling a bit of a coming home. This luxury allows me the beauty of sitting in silence, reflecting on my world, pulling out a life's lesson, lovingly coddling, sculpting the words on the page and maybe even touching your heart with my thoughts. Another non-negotiable...for the love.

Today, I want you to think about your identity as you answer the questions:

1. Who are you really?
2. What do you want to be known for and what are you doing about it?
3. Jump back on the bandwagon and make it all count...every minute. Only you can make this thing happen. Only you can choose your essential you.
4. If you aren't sure, give *something* a try...I dare you! Your identity may come bubbling to the surface as you honor your true self.

Day 3: Because There Really is *No One* Else

We tend to *put off* important things and *shy away* from really big things with the misguided thought that someone else will do it. Or worse, that we aren't qualified or called or "quite ready". Truthfully, most of these are glorified excuses. Excuses that get us out of the line of fire. Excuses that keep us in our comfort zone.

Each one of us is the sum total of our God-given talents, genetics, nurturing choices, and experiences. Each one of us has a unique combination of stuff that sets us up perfectly to be exactly who we are destined to be. Absolutely nothing, no experience is wasted. Wrestling with my own calling and personal set of assigned duties, though, I am starting to see how very important the true understanding of this really is. This gives me great comfort in my calling and motivation to press on.

When I think about what I am called to do, I can clearly see that *only I* am fit for the job. I don't mean that in an arrogant way. There is no one who sees the world exactly the way I do, no one who has all the exact life experiences that I do. And likewise, for you. There is no one who can fulfill *your* role exactly like you do, or complete the mission that you are called to.

Rest assured that you are not distinctly qualified to do *every* job and that you have permission to *say no*. There are many things that I do so poorly that it would be ridiculous for me to undertake them, and so, I embrace my talents humbly and do what I can with the skills that I have.

Knowing that I am the only one to whom this particular inspiration has visited in this particular way, I take it very seriously and with the utmost care. For many reasons, we have *every* right to shy away, be scared, overwhelmed, and lose hope. It is actually for all those reasons, that we dare not give up. We simply put one foot in front of the other and move forward, trusting that grace, wisdom, and peace will also come along for the ride.

Will you join me on this journey? I know that there is something special that is calling to you and *only you*. Maybe you are wishing that you made more time for it, hoping that you don't get scared or too busy to get to it. *That* is the thing that you must do. For there really is no one more qualified. No one. You are it and yes, *of course*, you are ready.

1. Is there something that you are avoiding or find yourself so overwhelmed with that you are not tackling it?
2. Be honest now. Looking at all your experience, your knowledge, your passion for that specific thing…is there anyone else who could do this?
3. If you could do one thing, forsaking all else, paid, or unpaid…what would it be?
4. This is your permission slip…Get to it!!

Day 4 - What Feels Effortless Even When it is Hard?

One of the keys to understanding what you *should* be doing, is to get super familiar and comfortable with what comes easily to you. Many people get so wrapped up in pursuing the American Dream at all costs, they forget to ask if what they are doing is really something that they love or have a natural ability for. They are missing the thing that makes them great *inherently*. Or, we get so wrapped up in the business of our vocation, we forget why chose the gig in the first place.

Here's an example: Many doctors I know spend an inordinate amount of time learning the business side of their practice. Their true talents lie in all the almost infinite facets of patient care, and yet, they spend crazy amounts of time learning business. The truth is, that they may be better served hiring all of it out, while they focus on patient care. Hiring it out to people that not only know the nuances, but have natural talents or propensities to excel at the business.

There is a bigger reason why you want to do this than simply the talent or propensity, though. It can be very expensive in terms of your life energy to spend hours, weeks, days, and ultimately a lifetime, doing something that is not really your jam. And let's face it, your life energy is the most important thing and most *expensive* thing that you can spend.

Before you go any further with your goal setting, spend some time working out what really makes your heart sing. The things that make you super happy and keeps you mentally healthy. The things to which you normally gravitate. The things you would do for free.

Then try to build your goals, your dreams, around those things.

If you really listen to your heart, it will come naturally. The trouble is, most professionals and entrepreneurs are so accustomed to disciplining themselves and delaying gratification, that they forget they could actually do something that they truly enjoy.

And yes, especially for a living.

1. Take some time & and craft the perfect day...what exactly would you be doing?
2. Have you put off doing what you want to do in favor of doing what you should do? Has that worked to bring you joy?
3. How might you better "marry" what you *want* to do with that which pays the bills?
4. Make a list of simple changes can you can make today.

Day 5: The Perfect Day

Let's look a little closer at the concept of *the perfect day*. I have done this exercise personally, with my patients and with coaching clients and the results are nothing short of astonishing. Use your imagination to picture yourself in the exact setting, lifestyle, environment that you would deem *perfect*.

The only rules? There has to be some viable work involved. That is, a sustainable lifestyle that includes a purposeful mission. So, in other words, while it may *seem* like your perfect life might be to live permanently on some idyllic island, (for me somewhere tropical), wiling the days away with spa treatments and never-ending shopping trips...this is neither sustainable, or nor purposefully missioned.

In this "perfect day" you have the academic degree that you covet, you have the house that suits you and your family perfectly, and you go to work at the vocation of your dreams. Why include work? Because we were built for it.

Made in the image of God, our bodies, and our minds were designed not only to move, but to actually do some sort of *productive* activity. If we are kept away from doing this for any reason, a part of us withers, we become in-grown, we get heart-sick, and our soul cannot thrive. So, for this exercise, your perfect day needs to include viable work.

This is what I found in almost every case: Most people are actually living very close to the life of their dreams. Maybe we wish that we were the lawyer instead of the paralegal, or maybe we love the work we are currently doing and just would just like to be acknowledged or paid a bit more. We love our house, but we just wish we had one more bedroom, a larger deck, or a more convenient laundry room.

Now, it can be argued that perhaps our imaginations are not creative enough to go much beyond the life we live right now. Or maybe, we have actually created a life that is very close to the life of our dreams, but we've merely hit some obstacles. This is probably more accurate.

So, today, don't be afraid to take a few moments to do this. Hone in on your *perfect day*. Then set about the process of making it happen. Right now. This is your one life. You get to choose what you will do with it.

1. Get super-specific about your perfect day.
2. Take steps to make it happen.
3. Review your day & and see how close you got...then celebrate when you hit it!

Day 6 - Do You Deserve Pleasure?

We sometimes act like we have no business enjoying our life. It is easy to get too busy to cultivate pleasure for its own sake. We forget how important it is to nurture ourselves with the wholesome activities that we *genuinely* enjoy.

In <u>The Pleasure Prescription: To Love, to Work, to Play</u>, Dr. Paul Pearsall explains the importance of nurturing pleasure so that we cannot only be fully alive, but that we might thrive. I am convinced that when we are fully healthy, we are better prepared to endure the "unenjoyable" things that will inevitably come.

I am not talking about falling into a fully hedonistic lifestyle that is consumed with *false pleasure. That* will surely fail to make us healthier. I am talking about deep, self- nurture that bolsters us up from the inside out. The idea here is to create such a strong foundation that even when the storms come, and they will, we will sail right through undaunted.

So, what is pleasure? Dictionary.com defines pleasure as enjoyment or *satisfaction* derived from what is to one's liking. Another definition quite simply: gratification. And yet another: delight.

I personally love being delighted. Anything that brings delight...literally *of the light,* is a very good thing. Pleasure done right, brings more light. More light into our lives, into those lives with whom we interact. More light for the world to share.

Why, then, do we shy away from pleasure? Especially among the strait-laced and ultra-successful, *too much pleasure* could not possibly be considered a good thing. We learn early on, to put off our own happiness, to delay gratification in the interest of whatever we must accomplish in the moment.

I am learning that seeking some form of healthy pleasure is not only very good, but necessary. Necessary if we want to *sustain* a high level of performance. And necessary if we are serious about bringing more light into the world.

I will admit that this is a really hard shift for me. I have lived most of my life denying myself of extravagant pleasures. Admittedly, I am not really given to much luxury. I don't really care about being pampered and I am definitely not into the status of such things. Honestly, I'd rather work. Crazy, I know, but true.

I can hum along quite happily when I have a lot to do, to put in order, to organize and get done. I can stay up late, grind it out and accomplish much. I actually love this feeling more than anything else. Looking back over all I have done and basking in the satisfaction of a job well done can keep me very happy, *almost indefinitely*. Almost. When it catches up with me, though, I have the realization that I am not really enjoying the fruits of all my hard labor at all.

Realizing that I haven't done anything remotely luxurious lately, not even having taken the most meager of vacations, in a really long time, I tend to get resentful. I resent that I haven't done more or maybe *anything*, for myself, as I selflessly serve others, the greater good, or whatever cause I am championing.

While I am accomplishing much, my soul is being drained of very life! Here is where I find that I should have tuned into pleasure. I should have paid attention. I should have looked at what I needed and why. As I have learned this, I have gotten better at observing and tuning into pleasures along the way. And as I do so, I am learning that I become better at my work and more productive in the trenches.

Enter the "sunset walk". I started this ritual a few years back upon returning home from a lovely vacation. I noticed that while on vacation, we made it a point to watch the sunset everyday. That is, we actually scheduled other activities around the sunset. I also noticed that I rarely do this at home. Upon further analysis, I saw that one of the main reasons, is that I can't see the sun *set* from my house. I have to walk up and over a large hill to see the horizon.

So, here's is what I did. I made a commitment with myself to do exactly that - walk over the hill to see the horizon – as often as I could. Now, rain or shine, I head out the door with my dog to watch my beloved sunset. The pleasure is so profound (and presumably mood-changing) that my kids have been known to physically shoo me out the door at the first hint of a pink sky.

My intrinsic reward, is that I come back refreshed, renewed, and re-set. Ready to tackle the next round of tasks, no matter how formidable.

Maybe, like me, you need to adopt a sunset walk, or your version of it. I challenge you to really think about the simple things in life that give you *great* pleasure, and make them part of your days. That is, to make an effort everyday, to be *delighted*. God created you to not only be productive, but to enjoy all of His blessings and all the beautiful pleasures that He provides.

Permission granted. And yes, you do deserve it.

1. What small, but effective, indulgences can you carve into your workday?
2. Is there an activity that fully nurtures you, fills you with pleasure?
3. What might you eliminate to make more room for pleasure in your life?

Day 7 - Celebrating the Day

There is always something to celebrate, something to be thankful for. Gratitude creates an energy that keeps us going. Celebration gives us *good reason* to enjoy the journey.

Fear, anxiety, sadness, defeat, or anger can always motivate me in the short term. It seems that one of the best ways I know to alleviate anxiety is to go to work. But the trouble is, when I arrive at the goal, guess what is there to meet me? You guessed it: All those same emotions.

Unless I learn and practice changing my mindset and processing these emotions, they will linger and likely fester. Furthermore, my brain will become wired for this tried-and-true emotional response...no matter what the circumstance.

If you are feeling an overall dissatisfaction with the results you are creating, feeling like you aren't doing enough or second-guessing your actions and results, please know that this is not coming from the results you are producing. Your results are likely *not deficient,* even if it may feel like it! The dissatisfied feeling is coming from how you are *thinking about your results.* All the thoughts and emotions that you are allowing along the way.

Here's the thing. Learning how to enjoy and celebrate every moment and then to truly enjoy the journey, will take an immense amount of pressure off the outcome. If you are able to enjoy the process of getting to your goal, even if it's hard, makes your life way more fun. And getting to the actual goal will become a bonus!

If you allow the destination to be charged with the task of *rescuing you* from the process, or yourself, what should be a joy-filled destination will likely suck the life out of the process, even if you manage to hit the goal. If we can, however, learn to celebrate our successes along the way, we will add some joy to the journey, and ultimately, we cannot lose.

Celebrating even the simplest victories, creating reasons to celebrate, taking time to appreciate the goodness in our lives, sets us up to receive more of the same. That means more victory, more celebration. Not only that, but life in celebration is just way more fun. It not only keeps us in the right mindset, but motivated each step of the way.

Celebrate life, the simple things, and all the beautiful people in your life. All of this becomes the rocket fuel to go for the next goal. If you don't reward yourself for a job well done, if you don't enjoy the simple things, life becomes a very tough taskmaster. Rather than motivating and freeing you to pursue the life of your dreams, your goals will feel more like a *noose* around your neck. And yes, I have been there. I have to remind myself often, to do this. Not only to stop and smell the roses, but to actually treat myself to some.

Let's be honest. There are days when I feel like I have *nothing* to be thankful for. It seems that nothing is going right and I am merely surviving. Unfortunately, this keeps me from accomplishing the very things that I need to do, to feel like I am accomplishing and moving forward.

If you find that you are often *not happy* with the results you create, you might need to do some work around changing your brain patterns. It is definitely worth the effort.

1. How might you build celebration into your *each* and every day?
2. Is there something specific that you take for granted in your process, that you could have more gratitude for?
3. When was the last time you acknowledged yourself for a specific skillset or ability? Take some time right now to do so.

STAYING IN THE GAME

5

Who Are Your People?

Now it is time to consider the people around you. Have you ever noticed that there are those in your life who are able to bring the best out in you? They motivate you to do your best work.

There are also those in your life who may not bring out the best in you. They suck the life out of you. They demand your time. They don't recognize that you have goals. They see you as a means to their ends, and what you can do for them.

Are certain friends and family members coming to mind?

How do we identify the people that we want and need around to support us? Is is it possible to be on the look-out for them, even before you get yourself into a soul-sucking pattern? I believe that it is not only possible. It is necessary.

Here is the thing. We tend to get into relationships that are both comfortable and rewarding for us. If we think about our natural tendency to avoid pain or relish pleasure, then take it a step further and determine what the payoff might be in each of our relationships.

No matter how special, please know that your colleagues are on their *own* journey and will probably not walk alongside you for long. Honestly, I have spent way too much time trying to keep all my beloved people right beside my journey with me.

Trying to keep them happy, garnering their support or help, making sure they are comfortable and satisfactorily occupied while I am busy with this or that, takes bandwidth that I really don't have to spare. Hanging around on *my* adventure is not that fun for them and probably a waste of energy for me.

This week, we are not only going to investigate *who* our people are, but why we gravitate towards them. It is time to get around the people that nurture you and your most important goals.

Day 1 - People-Pleasing

For those of us who are people pleasers, we know how addictive it can be. To feel that dopamine hit when you make someone smile with your efforts, to save the day, to help them meet their goals.
Don't get me wrong, helping is a very noble pursuit. But when helping everyone else comes at the *expense* of your own goals, or as an *excuse* to not pursue your own passion projects, it can be a very real problem.

Clearly, we want people around who bring out the best in us.

Why is it then, that you find yourself caught up in relationships that not only suck the life out of you, but rob you of your mission?
It seems that there is might be something in us that honors *their* mission over ours. Maybe because our thing spends so much time in our heads, it becomes over-familiar and maybe even a bit lack-luster. Is it possible that they sell us on their mission to a greater degree than we can sell ourselves on our own?

We are born with a fantastic sense of self. We just *know* that we can do anything that we put our minds to, before we know anything else. If we are lucky, we have parents that back up our inner knowing, by encouraging us keep believing. Knowing that someone believes in us whole-heartedly, goes a long way in fostering confidence. If we could simply take that and run with it, we would probably encounter far fewer obstacles later in life.

For most of us, though, the journey is a bit more complicated. I had a truly wonderful childhood. However, even while I was taught that I could do or become anything I put my mind to, I was also taught to not to think too big, to rein in the really crazy ambitions and try to conform to what is 'normal'. Thankfully, I still believe to this day that I can do anything that I put my mind to. At the same time, though, I tend to rein in the fun, the extravagance, *the crazy*. Funny how sticky that early influence is.

This has probably served at times to keep me grounded and I would also guess that it has limited me. One of my mom's favorite sayings was, "after laughing comes crying!"...And you guessed it, I learned to never laugh too hard or too long. It seemed to me that the harder I laughed, the higher the risk that there would be some cosmic heck to pay.

In other words, if I kept my fun, my joy, to a minimum, always work before play, I would be safe and everything would be fine.

So, maybe your brand of control is slightly different than mine. I would venture a guess, though, that there is something within you that wants to rebel against the constant changes of the day-to-day. Rather than embracing change, we cling to age-old traditions, the status quo, and the way things have always been. To safety.

This is one of the many reasons we need an exquisite support system. People that not only believe in us, but challenge us and help us to be our very best. They say that behind every good man is a strong woman, a praying woman, a supportive woman, and a patient one. I would take it a step further and ask you to think about who you would love to have *beside* you, not behind.

As you work through the questions for today, think about building your support network and the exact who that you need in your corner to help you achieve your goals and dreams....

1. Name three people in your life that always encourage and believe in you.
2. Name three people that always seem to "'rain on your parade.'"
3. Take active steps to foster the encouraging relationships.
4. Decide how you might limit exposure to the nay-sayers.

Day 2 - Mentors

I have always loved the idea of being taken under someone's wing and taught, raised up, discipled. There is a certain coziness, almost romanticism, that someone would care this much for another's success. I have had wonderful mentors throughout my childhood, college years, and in graduate school. Teachers, coaches, pastors that unselfishly poured into my life.

Upon graduation and settling into the rhythm of my own private practice, however, I began to realize how much harder it was to foster those types of relationships. Now, it seemed, I was to have it all figured out. I was in the position to be the mentor. After being the consummate student for most of my life, this was not a position that I was accustomed to. It drove me to read, study, and learn as much as I could in the areas like clinical practice, self-help, psychology, and peak performance.

After 29 years of practice, my drive to learn is still going strong. They are all mentoring me. And while I may never meet those authors or podcasters in person, I feel like many have guided and taught me as though we were in a private tutorial or coaching session.

As I am being mentored, I mentor. I share the knowledge, the enlightenment, my growth with anyone and everyone who is willing to listen. Thankfully, people are pretty gracious about hearing me out. Usually, if I do it right, I provide value. Then, if they put it in practice, they see breakthroughs. I love the ripple effect.

So it is with you. We *all* encounter mentors, whether we realize it or not. We take what we have learned and we either run with it or walk away unchanged. You have a choice to run with what you are learning or stagnate.

I encourage you to stay in a stance of availability, openness, a stance of complete , readiness. Always. This is just one way that we can learn from almost any experience. I was astonished when I learned that my all-knowing grandfather tried to learn something every day. Imagine if we were that available to learn new things. Imagine if we could not only learn something new every day, but implement that new knowledge. Be open to learning and available to be taught. When the student is ready, the teacher will appear. Always.

1. Who are you learning from?
2. Who would you like to be learning from?
3. How can you make that happen?
4. Think of ways that you might connect with a mentor of your dreams...

Day 3 - What Are We Learning From Our Mentors?

We often overlook exactly how much we are influenced by the people around us. If we enjoy them, we leave it at that, not realizing that the subtle influences affect our thinking and our behavior. Most of the time, this influence is for good.

We can usually identify toxic relationships before they destroy us, particularly if the influence is strong. We can generally remove ourselves, or create a distance before they wreak havoc over our lives. But, what if the influence is subtle? What if it creeps in, bit-by-bit, so insidiously, that you don't notice the damage it until is too late?

It is that influence that I want to speak to today. You may be in a relationship that is shaping your identity, your work, your life in a way that is no longer serving you. You may even recognize that this friend is taking you down a road that you really don't want to travel. You may have unsuccessfully tried to extricate yourself. And you may be using this influence as an excuse not to pursue your calling, your dreams, and your highest aspirations.

As a bona fide people pleaser, I have personally spent many years helping other people achieve their goals and dreams, while my very own lay neglected, ignored, and forgotten. What I have discovered is this: It is a long and winding road back. Long, because I literally had to extricate myself from their dream-works. Winding, because I found myself falling regularly, and quite readily, back into the old pattern.

It has become a bit of a mantra now to "choose me today". Not in a selfish way, but in a nurturing way. Making my calling a priority, so that I catch myself, lest I fall into using someone else's goals as a great excuse not to pursue my own.

See, when you have a big job or goal or aspiration in front of you, it can actually take less emotional investment to lose yourself in taking on *their* goals. It is, in a sense, the easy way out. Not that their dreams and goals are any easier or take less energy. (You may be just as spent at the end of the day!)

When we have less to lose, less emotional connection, it is easy to fall into theirs and completely forget about our own, while giving ourselves a very viable and ready excuse.

The thinking and justification might sound something like this: Theirs needs to be done right now. Yours can wait. And therefore, yours will wait.

I contend, though, yours will *not* wait forever. Denied long enough, your passion will eventually run out. Often, along with all your energy.

Hope deferred makes the heart sick, but when the desire comes, it is a tree of life.

—-Proverbs 13:12

For me, the real toll it takes is the eventual resentment that I feel at the end of a long week of denying myself all of my own attention. This wears away at the fabric of my very soul. The chronic self-denial grates on me at the very core of who I am.

In fact, given enough time, I forget who I really am, as I get caught up in all the other roles that I am playing. Not to mention that forgetting about myself ends up stealing my joy. This is a slippery slope. And and one that *can* be avoided.

The choice is always ours to make. Every day, no matter how noble the hard work you are doing for for others might be, you must *choose you*. Choose to nurture yourself, your inner calling, your inner light. Choose to be the person God created you to be. And then choose to help, but do not be consumed for a minute by someone else's real estate.

Choose to love, always, but don't stop pursuing your own dreams.

1. Are you learning anything from the people that are nearest and dearest to you?

2. Are you allowing them to be too much in charge, so that you have lost agency or authority over your own life?
3. What might you want to do differently? I encourage you to make those hard choices today.

Day 4 - Who are You Mentoring?

We must push ourselves to interact. In a world of social distancing and masks, we have to be purposed about this. Those who live in seclusion tend to get increasingly comfortable there. And increasingly less comfortable around people. The longer we give in to this comfort zone, the easier it is to make excuses as to why you should stay home and not interact with anybody.

A few weeks ago, as I was wrapping up with a patient, he said,"You knew what to do, from the first minute you saw me!" I was more than a bit confused. At the same time, I was flattered that he would think that much of my diagnostic and clinical skill, so, of course, I asked what he meant.

"I will never forget that day. You were laser-focused on me. I knew that you had my number." I laughed, trying to recall what in the world he was talking about. He explained how he had been suffering with inexplicable aches and pains, feeling terrible all the time. He hypothesized that he was just getting older, even though admittedly, it kind of scared him. He was at a loss as to what he should be doing about it.

We were at a Spinal Screening event when we met that day, and I honestly don't remember the laser-like focus nor *having his number*. What I do remember, though, is the intention that always accompanied those events.

"There is always at least one person we meet that desperately needs us, has tried everything, that quite literally does not know what to do about their condition. I think on that day, that person was you." I answered him with sincerity, as it really did happen every time.

He began to tear up. "You guys have helped me so much. I can't believe the difference. You fixed a problem I didn't even know I had. I feel better now, younger than I did all those years ago...and I am 10 years older!"

I am often baffled when people remind me of something I said or did years ago, that was life-changing. As iron sharpens iron, we influence those with whom we share a community, whether we realize it or not. See, there is no reason to stress over whether or not you are capable of making an impact. If you simply make yourself available and become aware of those around you, you will bring light and life to your world everywhere you go. But, go you *must*.

I was just fulfilling a commitment that day that I had made months before. I wasn't looking for him, but he was unwittingly looking for us. We connected. His life changed. It is so simple, really.

We tend to over-complicate this. We tend to think that we have nothing to offer. Until we offer it, that is. Until we simply do the thing we are meant to do and somebody's life is changed.

So, get out and do it. Do your job. Love somebody.

Fear not, for I am with you. I will never leave nor forsake you.
---Isaiah 40:11

1. Are you regularly connecting with people?
2. How might you up your "connection game?"
3. Reflect back on a time when you really touched someone deeply with something that seemed quite ordinary for you.
4. Journal what you learned about your calling in that experience.

Day 5 - If You Were the Last Man on Earth...

Here is an interesting idea to toss around. What if you were the last person on the planet and it was your job to leave a legacy? A body of work that sums up all the things you have learned and want to pass along. What if it was up to you to train up the next generation? What if there was no one else to do this for you?

Clearly, this would add a measure of urgency that we don't often contemplate. Put another way, what if today was your very last chance to get it right? To do the thing that you were put here to do.

It is so easy to get complacent and forget how very fleeting our precious life really is. If you're anything like me, you forget that every day we spend doing anything other than what we really *want* to do, are *called* to do...is time that we will never get back. That is enough to give me some serious chills.

If that is not enough, think about the people. What about those whom you might have touched, coached, healed, or taught? I know, this is a lot to think about. It might feel really heavy. And that's okay.

I want you to feel the mantle of your calling. There is no one else who can do this thing quite like you. We forget how amazing we really are, how significant, unique and exactly how critical our contribution might be.

Today, I want you to think about your legacy and those whom God has allowed you to reach. Take a moment and pray for those you have *yet* to reach and then sit back for a moment and listen.

1. What do you think God would tell you to do with your time?
2. Can you do some of that today?
3. Take a good look at your schedule and modify accordingly.
4. How do you really *want* to spend your time?

Day 6. Who is Listening to You?

It struck me today that not everyone is interested in what I have to say. And, I really am okay with that. Not everyone is interested in Oprah Winfrey, either, (and she is pretty interesting!) Most people have a measure of interest and, not in a bad way, tune me out when they reach their limit. We all do this. And then there are those who really care. Over the past two days, I have had three people ask me if I am writing. Thank you and *bless* you if you have ever asked a writer if they are writing!

I am a bit bowled over by it to be honest.

First, that they are interested and secondly, that they care. It is for you that I am persevering. But alas, it is also for me. Here is the cool thing. They all reminded me of that fact, in some way. That I need to keep writing...for me.

They all know how much this means to me and that I am more fully *me* when I am writing. They also recognize how much it means to you, the reader. The things you have read *changed you* in some way, and so you all cheer me on.

Today, I needed to hear that. I could have survived without the encouragement, but I don't know if I would have shown up on the page. Eventually, I would have circled back here, I always do. Understand, though, your words, have power. Your love and your concern gave me the motivation I needed to stay in the game, with a full heart.

So, keep reminding me even as I keep reminding you. I want you to stop at nothing to reach your goals. I want to cheer you on from the sidelines. I want you to have this same fullness of heart. I want you to have the joy of seeing things come to fruition, as you execute your labor of love. Just be reminded that not everyone cares. And that is okay. There will always be some who really do care and those *are* your people. Don't ever forget them. They love you for who you are, exactly the way you are. Right now. No improvements necessary. And they want the best for you. They will help you become more fully you.

Don't try and convince those that don't care. This is a losing battle and a bit of a fool's mission. A waste of precious time. Declare your message, live your dream, pursue your goals with tenacity and passion and your people will back you up. The apathetic and the haters will will go on doing what they have always done and probably suck the life out of you. Speaking to them will only dilute your message and make you miserable. You have one chance to live today.

Don't you dare get distracted by the opinions of others. I promise you, it is a losing game. You can't please everyone, and you can't please anyone all of the time. It isn't even worth the effort. Take time to hear from God, listen to your heart and then live your life in obedience to Him. Your message will come out loud and clear.

Don't you dare shrink away from your calling. Be on the lookout for encouragement. There are people who will support you. They are worth the effort and so are you.

Now go and do likewise. You got this.

1. Think of at least three people who have cared enough to encourage you in your life.
2. How can you spend more time or re-connect with them?
3. What would they encourage you to do more of today? Go and do it.

Day 7 - You Never Know...Keep Saying Thank You

There is so much despair in the world. So much angst, frustration, anger, and plain old sadness. If you take the time to notice, you can see it in the eyes of almost everyone with whom you rub shoulders. You likely feel it wafting off your own family members like a bad smell. It is all around us and yet, the despair is often only one tiny step away from completely *reversing* itself. The magic elixir against despair is often as simple as embracing sincere gratitude. Easier said than done, right?

Sometimes I can embrace gratitude from a very rosy place. At times, it seems I have so very much to be thankful for, that I wonder what there is to be sad about. In those times, I can easily pull myself up out of my funk by my own bootstraps and get on with it.

On the other hand, what about the times when you don't feel there is anything or any reason at all to be thankful. What then? This is actually where a gratitude practice can really work for you. *This* is where thanksgiving can do its *best* work. It has been said that gratitude and depression cannot co-exist. Gratitude and anxiety do not mix well either. Gratitude puts you in an energy of can do. It gives you hope. Gratitude restores the most basic foundation of faith to our fragile, broken souls; often giving us the motivation to hang on for one more day.

However, what if everything seems hopeless, right now? What if everything you are doing seems to only bring on more frustration, angst, and anger? I get it, and I see you. I have definitely been there.
I want to propose this as a contrasting possibility...What if all that you are going through is not only exactly right, but right on time?

For me, that means that I can say thank you, today, no matter how murky the cesspool. If I know that the hard stuff is a way for me to move forward. If I know that this discomfort is my ticket to something better; if I can trust that this state, right here and right now is temporary, (it always is) I can genuinely be thankful. I can trust that my life will get better. Or at the very least, different.

Tomorrow will be a new day. Tomorrow will give you another chance. Saying thank you today, can propel you to that new place just a little quicker. And maybe with a bit more happy momentum. Being thankful when we don't feel like it, is probably the work of our lives. Being thankful will dig you out of your pit. Staying thankful will keep you from falling in, in the first place.

Start with the basics. Take a look around and cultivate gratitude. For the simplest of things, for clean air, water, a house to live in. Family, health, and food to eat.

I'm thankful for the rain that forces me inside today that I might focus on writing and reading (two of my most favorite things), and cleaning my house. It's just that easy!

I am thankful for hard lessons that make me stronger. For all *the hard* that I have gone through to get here. I am who I am because I have toiled, I have been in pain. I have survived.

I am thankful for *the hard* today which will complete its work in me, even today.

1. Write a Gratitude List for the Hard Things.
2. Start a Daily Gratitude Practice.
3. Observe and Journal what happens to your mood when you are genuinely thankful.

6

What is Your Why?

This week we are going to focus on the reason you do what you do. Having a strong *why* will help you stay motivation through the highs and the lows. Understanding the real reason you do what you do will give you every reason in the world to keep going. This might very well be your most important work, not only to understand it, but to allow that *why* to carry you.

Take time to do the necessary work, this week. Answer the questions thoughtfully.

Sometimes, it is good to answer with the most top-of-mind ideas, but don't take any of this work lightly. Your life really does depend on this.

Don't short-change who you are for a minute.

Let's get to it!

Day 1 - How Do You Know That it is the *Right* Game?

We cannot expect to go from mountaintop to mountaintop, no matter what goal you we are pursuing. No matter how much you love it. There is always the dull, mundane, hard, and sometimes horrifically bad that we have to work through, to stay in any game. For a long time, I have bought into the reasonable notion that if everything is going smoothly, then I must be doing something right.

The reverse, then, also had be true, if I encountered an obstacle, some uphill battle, some challenge that seemed insurmountable, then I was very obviously on a very wrong track. I had better course-correct. Something went wrong, I had gotten off track.

Some would claim that an opposing take is actually truer. And that is, if I am encountering trouble, some evil force has recognized my potential for good and is working hard to stop me. Evil wants to derail me *before* I have a chance to change the world for the better. Our job, at least in part, is to show that we are in the game for the long haul. At any cost, no matter what.

When all things line up conveniently and everything purrs along, as though by some inspired and divine design, it makes me think that I am doing exactly the right thing and God is in agreement with me. At other times, those opposing forces seem to oppose simply for the sake of it. How I work through those difficulties can actually define me. Those difficulties help us to become who we are. The truth is, we will always have some of both. There will be the good, the bad and the ugly...no matter what you choose to put your hand to.

So, I think it is important as you contemplate your *why*, to consider the downside as well as the upside. I have been very blessed with a very busy professional life. The downside is that I don't have time or energy to devote to many aspects of the practice that could use my expertise.

I get to choose. Sometimes I have to choose between good and better, or better and best. Do I dwell on my lack of time, rail against it, scream and yell? I am embarrassed to say that I have done all those things at times. I have made good choices but I have also squandered my time and energy. I am best served to simply let it go and move on to the next thing.

In the end, I think that moving on is what keeps me sane. Knowing that whatever had my attention for the moment, had it for a reason. I will do my best right now, learn from any mistakes and do it better next time. That sounds a bit cavalier, and I don't mean to be. What is to be gained by beating myself up over my short falls? I have done my share of that, to be sure. It is better to simply let it go.

When I am honest with myself, I have to admit that no matter how badly I mess up or how hard things get, I am willing get up the next morning and try again. What vocation or calling are you willing to get up and do, again and again, no matter how hard today? Ask yourself why.

1. How bad is the downside really? Could it be just as bad in another vocation?
2. How have you grown through the hard stuff?
3. Has it been worth it?

Day 2 - Once You have Found the *Right Game*

If you can answer that it is indeed worth it...that you will come back again and again, no matter what...you have indeed found a very good thing. It is time to dig in and make it happen. If you are anything like me, you may have put everything and everyone before your own choices and often before your own happiness. Maybe it is super-hard for you to even contemplate the life of your dreams, let alone the *dream* of your dreams.

Please do not despair. You belong here. I am convinced that by staying in your current game, you can show the world and yourself, once and for all, that you are deserving of a bigger or even a completely different game.

Think back to grade school. We were all required to put in our time before we go headed off to college or the various vocations that we chose. None of us could honestly say that we wish we were back there, getting teased on the playground or cramming for finals in a shared college dorm. And yet, we learned that we had to put in our time, knowing it was a steppingstone to a better place. This place.

Thinking back over all the hours of plodding through undergrad classes and then graduate school, memorization of minutia, grueling study, it taught me patience and perseverance and how to make the best of things, no matter what. So it goes in real life.

No matter what your calling, there will be things that you don't love about it. All these challenges add up to a life well-lived, no matter how much it might feel like the exact opposite. How do you know that you are in the right game? How do you know that you might not be, but instead have passed the point of no return? Maybe you feel like you have to stay right where you are, stuck here, no options. At least for now.

The truth is that sometimes you just don't know if it is the right game. While it is true that almost any game is better than none, it is worth taking some time to determine if what you are doing is really the best use of your time. Any game is healthier than sitting on the sidelines wondering if you qualify, wondering if you are good enough. Wondering what you should be doing and if you are risking the wasting of your life.

If you have come this far, I am going to contend that you belong. I hereby grant you permission to be here. It seems sometimes that we have been chosen, that somehow our profession chose us. I also think that if you have not deliberately chosen it back, you may still be on the sidelines, wondering, wandering. Today, I dare you to choose it back. Wholeheartedly. Choose now and don't look back.

1. Why are you in the game?
2. If you feel that it chose you, have you chosen it back?
3. Whether you are in the right game or not, how could you tweak your game to make it suit you more closely?

Day 3 - Does it Make Your Heart Sing?

I am convinced the most important thing in finding the right game is how your heart feels when you are in it. Does it delight you? Does it make you really, really happy? I have spent most of my life working at something that I legitimately enjoy. As a business owner for most of that time, I have been able to do it mostly on my terms. There have been really great times, but there have also been really rocky times. Because I love the work and the philosophy behind what I do, it has been a very positive career choice.

When the rough times hit, it is my love for the game that keeps me going. So it must be with your passion project. If you can love it enough, even the hardest times will become easier to handle. Your appreciation for the process required to make progress is pretty important, too. If you can love the process enough, you will never have to work a day. As you engage in the process, progress will take care of itself.

I have taught myself, trained myself to love the process of things. With work, with our home, even with my hobbies. Yes, there are things that are not easily lovable, even with our hobbies that must be endured to get to the fun part.

However, there must be an easy love that is inherent, literally part of the activity that makes it worth doing for you. I challenge you to find it. If you are at a point where your passion project has become a bit of a grind, that is normal. Completely and totally. You have arrived.

Today, I challenge you to challenge yourself with this one. Take some time with these questions, get brutally honest with yourself. This is important work.

1. Do you genuinely love the process?
2. Do you love it so much that you want to do it even when the going gets tough

3. Does your work here energize you? If not, how can you shift to make this more fun? Do it today...it will be worth the effort.

Day 4 - Stop Feeling Shame

Guilt says I have done something wrong. Shame says I *am* wrong. Guilt can put you back on the right path. Shame can eat you alive. It can be an all-consuming, heart-wrenching, progress-stopping force that is paralyzing, if you let it. It will make you quit. *If you let it.*

Romans 8:1 says, *"Therefore, there is no condemnation to those who are in Christ-Jesus."*

I find myself whispering this, muttering this daily, throughout the day, as I navigate the minefields of criticism and self-condemnation. We are not called to this. We are called to live our lives to the best of our abilities, with the hope of Christ firmly planted in our hearts.

"It is for freedom that we have been set free." Paul admonishes in *Galatians 5:1.*

Not for the sake of bondage. Christians can so easily buy into the enemy's pack of lies. Although we have been set free, we place ourselves back into shame and bondage over the silliest of things.
"If only I could be a better mom, then I will write my book about it." We say.
"If only I could sell more widgets, then I would write my business handbook."
"If only I could be more perfect, then people will listen to me." (And we say *nothing* as we wait for perfection to come!)
All of that self-talk is thinly-veiled excuse-making. You will never be perfect enough to qualify as *the* expert. No one is. What we all need to know and can relate to, is how you kept yourself going in

the midst of your struggle. How you made it things happen in spite of the challenges and your very real and unique inadequacies.

I will confess that I feel guilty any time I choose my own stuff over my family and friends. What makes my goals more important than someone else's? Having grown up as a competitive figure skater, I remember well all the sacrifices my family made for me. For years it seemed, our life revolved around skating practices, competitions and the endless preparation for all of it.

I vowed that I would someday grow out of all that selfishness. I vowed that when I was fully grown up, I would focus on someone else's needs, desires, and goals. And so, somewhere during the process of growing up, I did just that. I decided that my goals were no longer the most important. If I was to be fully adult, I would need to *sacrifice* like my parents did. My goals and dreams would have to take a second seat to my husband's and my kids'. Not only that, I would find myself constantly asking, seeking out ways that I might help someone else achiever their goals, instead of "selfishly" focussing on mine.

You can probably guess what happened. As a result of helping everyone around me meet their goals, ignoring anything that might look or *seem* like it was important to me, I became in-grown, sad, frustrated. All my goals and dreams strangled...by my very own hand.

Is it wrong to sacrifice, to give up one's life for another? Absolutely not. Some say that this is the essence of being a true Jesus-follower. Is it wrong to give up one's hopes and dreams for those of another? Here's where it gets dicey. I believe that, at least in part, our deepest, most heartfelt hopes and dreams are *at one* with our calling. Those dreams and goals are given to you for a reason. This is what we were created to do. If we carelessly cast them aside, we might very well be giving up who we are meant to be. We may be giving up God's chosen thing for us, His will, the divine plan.

Being there, in a sacrificial way for family and friends, is not a bad thing. In fact, it is a truly noble thing to be able to put yourself aside for another. However, when I do this and only this, a very good thing can turn a bit sour. Over-achieving for others, while I become completely stifled, in-grown, and stagnant in my own stuff? This cannot possibly be a good thing for me or those I am "helping". For in doing so, I turn into someone that I definitely am not.

Today, I encourage you to think deeply about your very own goals and dreams and do something to pursue them. Whether it be a short workout, a significant phone call, sitting down at your computer, writing down the next most actionable steps. Whatever the case, do something that moves you in the direction of your dreams today. Yes, I mean that literally, do something that moves you. For we know that movement is life to your soul.

Your dreams and goals need to live and breathe and move. They need to be nurtured, paid attention to. Both for you and *everyone* around you.

Just know that by pushing past this barrier, you may inspire another to do the same. It is always worth the effort!

1. Take stock of what's on your To-Do list today.
2. Add one action step that moves you in the direction of your dreams.
3. Now, move. *Really.* Go ahead and do it. Permission granted.

Day 5 - Can You Go It Alone?

This is one of the things I most struggle with. It is often hard for me to do the solitude required to do this work. Sitting down at my computer by myself, seems too indulgent, almost too luxurious. Too much of a splurge of time, wasteful even. In black and white, even as I write this, I see the ridiculousness of that thinking. I have convinced myself that helping everyone else is *not* a waste of time, but doing something I enjoy, somehow...*is*.

It does help me, at times, to realize that I might actually be helping even more people, as I sit down to write. I have tried to think of myself as my own biggest charity case. And if that is the case, I am obligated to help myself. All this self-helpery should make me more sane, more able, more clear, and even more efficient, right? Trouble is, I don't really buy any of that.

The truth is that I write because I want to. And that, really is the most compelling *why* for me. I think we need to keep getting to the simple place of *want to*. That is, streamlining your life so that your most important *want to* becomes the priority.

I wonder why this is such a struggle for so many of us. This work is every bit as necessary as my breath. If I don't have productive work and contribution, that means something to me, I find that I shrivel, I become depressed, sick, ill-defined, and less effective. Sure, I can do the things I need to. I usually manage to get the gumption to fulfill my obligations. Is it my best work, though, when I don't bring my best self?

The idea here, is not only to keep moving forward, but to make your thing equally as important as everyone else's and then, moving forward and pushing through whatever is trying to stop you.

For me, I create my own worst resistance. It catches up with me though, whether in the moment or eventually. It catches up when I realize that I might be succumbing to the sickness of purpose-neglect. The sickness of not being in the moment, the sickness of longing for what is *really* real for me.

Here is the good news. The only way back is to simply get back to it. We tend to over-complicate this. For me, when I forget to define the essence of who I am and why I am here, I lose myself to the pull of the day.

So, I simply get back to writing and thinking. We must make a habit of getting down to the essence of things, to actually simplify the things that we tend to over-complicate and then actually get them done, in bite-sized pieces.

By staying distractedly busy, we are able to dodge the hard thing, the very thing we care about the most. By not facing it, we might escape the hard work for a moment. Rather than truly escaping, though, *the hard* usually gets more complicated and sometimes can become even harder.

So, today, I will face the music and go forward, not worrying about what I am not doing. Diagnosing and fixing me first, so that I can then serve you from a truly healthy place. And then, perhaps I can share what I learned on my journey.

Self-nurture, exquisite self-care, self-love, and abandonment to my purpose, all the things that add up to my best life, right now. Far from selfish, I can love the world with my gifts. So, all this "selfish" alone-time becomes a spring board from which I can share my best self.

Will you join me?

1. What activity are you truly gifted at and aspire to do more than anything else?
2. Is your *not* sharing your truth causing you more discomfort than if you did?
3. Do the work and take the time to congratulate and love yourself, today...You are not alone.

Day 6 - What Makes You Quit?

Now that we are getting somewhere. I think it is a good time to address the elephant in the room. We tend to stop ourselves, just when the "gettin' is good" Maybe not a universal trait, but common enough that it deserves mention.

J.D. Salinger, author of one of the most studied novels of all time, <u>Catcher in the Rye,</u> never published again, for fear that it could never be as good as his first novel.

We sit back and cry, "How could you?" Quit, that is. "When we just found you? Your most basic, even unedited musings would be beautiful and inspiring and worth the effort. Why stop now?"

Could it be a type of "Rockstar Syndrome"? That pesky condition that afflicts the ultra-successful and ultra-talented. It seems that just as quickly as the meteoric rise to fame, they systematically de-construct themselves and careen into a crash landing. Right back to where they started from. Lottery winners tend to do it too.

Is it a type of poverty complex? Certainly, it could be that, but it seems there is far more to it, than simply not being comfortable with our own success. Somewhere along the way, we stop doing the thing that leads to our greatness, that one thing that gives us the edge.

Maybe one of the reasons is that we tend to fear our own brilliance. We fear standing out. We fear beating out the next guy and ironically, we fear not living up to our own potential. My simple answer is this: Lighten up and get back to it.

Or maybe just lighten up. Period. Stop taking yourself so seriously. None of this matters all that much. The world, like it or not, doesn't really care that much about you. That sounds harsh, I know, but stressing over your own success, to your own detriment, is definitely not worth the energy. The world, most certainly, is not going to come and fetch you, dust you off or patch you back up, when you implode.

If you have had success in the past, I am going to humbly suggest that you stay with it. Keep on. You know what it takes, so carry on. Whatever your reason, I want you to simply stop *stopping* today. Keep at it because you love this thing. Because it loves you back. Especially when you nurture your talent enough to bring you success. And most importantly, because it is the right thing to do.

If you haven't been wildly successful in the past, I will give you the same advice. You may not know the specifics of what you need to do, but doing nothing…never got anyone anywhere.

Do what you do for the sake of it. Enjoy the nitty, gritty, the getting your fingernails dirty. Explore and enjoy your own magnificence and remember than that nothing will happen in your life, if you don't first choose to do something.

1. Have you caught yourself stopping or even slowing down, just when the 'gettin' is good'?
2. Are you ready to take it to the next level? Put your nose to the grindstone and get to it.
3. Think of one "Rockstar" whose work you miss right now, because they imploded or quit.
4. Stay the course. Finish the race.

Day 7 - Coming Home

I am a bit embarrassed to admit to this, but there are times when I take such prolonged breaks from my writing that the words on the page barely recognize me...or more accurately, I barely recognize them. As disheartening as that is, I realized again, today, that this is why I write. I didn't intend perfection when I set out to write this book, but I did intend to help us both stop quitting. I want you to know that I am right there with you and far from perfect in my own stoppage. You are not alone.

The thing that I have not done, is give up. Even when it seems like I have disappeared completely from this project, here I am, back at it again and ready for whatever God may lay on my heart to share. I am proud of myself for returning to it. I feel really good about swallowing my ego and humbly returning to the page. It feels like a "coming home".

Whatever it is that you are putting off, for whatever reason, I encourage you to come back and *just do it*! I like to think that my excuses are many and varied and generally quite good. I like to think that I am far more concerned about everyone else's happiness than my own.

To my credit, I might simply be too adaptable. I find genuine joy in serving and helping others find their joy. As the resident "happiness expert", it seems that I can effortlessly assist anyone whose bliss eludes them. Trouble is, it is not at all effortless, and over time, it comes at a huge expense.

No one can sacrifice forever, though, something has to give.

The hard realization is that my energy is not unlimited or free. And neither is yours. What I am slowly learning from my personal experience of self-sacrificing is that eventually I do wear out. And then, have nothing left for me.

If I am living, *instead*, from a place of being so filled up that I can't help but spread the love to everyone around me...this will be a different story. This happiness will be infectious.

So, what if, I was to live from the place of my purpose. What exactly would that look like? I actually feel a bit breathless when I think about it.

My true purpose in this life, is to glorify God. To draw others to Him. To not only be content, but to live with an unquenchable joy. *That* is what I want to be remembered for.

If we, as moms, parents, caregivers, dive deep into the things that bring us joy, we will all become a little bit better in all of our varied roles. We will have *more* to contribute to the mundane tasks of life. We can even learn to enjoy what we really don't normally enjoy, if we have saturated our souls with self-love and self-care.

1. Take baby steps today. Just start.
2. What scares you so much that you don't even want to try? Do *especially* that.
3. If this is something you need to go back to, go back like your life depends on it...

...Because it actually does. Welcome home.

7

Steps For Today

> *The moment one definitely commits oneself, then **providence** moves too. All sorts of things occur to help one that would never have otherwise have occurred...Unforeseen incidents, meetings and material assistance, which no man could have dreamed would have come his way.*
> --**J.W. Goethe**

Getting the job done pretty much comes down getting the job done. And while that might seem over-simplified, it is also the good news. Each step forward is *indeed* a step forward and while it might not be exactly what you might have hoped it would be, or everything you imagined, moving forward is the name of the game.

I encourage you to *Stay in The Game* this week by taking steps in the direction of your dreams. Don't you dare beat yourself up for what you aren't doing, but instead celebrate every minute of moving forward. You are a force to be reckoned with, if you only just allow yourself that distinction. Don't settle for a minute. You were made for this moment and you have everything within you to win the game. And anything else can be learned or delegated. You got this!

Day 1: But I Don't Want to Get Out of Bed.

We just got a brand-new bed and it is outdoing itself. As a result, I don't want to leave it. Why would I? I might also be lingering horizontal today because I may have stayed up too late reading. Okay, admittedly, I just started a novel, and like the new bed, I don't want to leave it either.

So, I have to make a choice. Do I languish in bed or face the day?

Well, truthfully, there are days when I would be perfectly content doing just that, wiling away the days with a good book and a hot cup of coffee. However, to stay right here and accomplish *nothing* does not sit well with me, either. And while that seems idyllic, it is not something that I could actually do for very long.

As I try to put my work off further, my mind drifts back to a conversation that I had with one of my favorite patients, Cletis. His joyful demeanor is a breath of fresh air. You would never know that he spends his days *and* nights serving his dear wife as her full-time caregiver. This is a true marvel to me, considering the energy required to meet the demands of the 24/7 round-the-clock care-taking.

When I asked him what keeps him vibrant, alive, and happy after all these years, he replied, with no hesitation, "Well, I am fulfilling a promise that I made over 60 years ago."

Whoa. Mic drop.

Please understand that although his decision 60 years ago might have been simple and straightforward, the day-to-day grind of living with the end stages of Alzheimer's is anything but. The simplicity of his resolve left me a bit speechless.

He likely would not be able to face the world with so much positivity, if he was wallowing in self-pity or questioning his purpose. This reminds me that I do what I do, because I made a commitment to do it. Whatever the goal, formally or informally, we make commitments and promises to ourselves.

It seems that when it comes to creativity or passion projects, all the rules change. We think we can somehow get away with putting them off. However, every time we break those commitments, every time we fail to meet our own personal goals, we lose a bit of ourselves. Over time, the damage can be catastrophic.

See, when it comes to work or home projects, eventually, we have to get around to do the actual work. There are bills to pay, children to feed, a house to keep up. It all needs attention or life will begin to unravel. If neglected, entropy will have the last word.

Although we often fail to see it this way, the same is true of our goals and dreams. If you neglect them long enough, they too will go away. The fire will eventually go out, your passion will disappear. Your energy will be so diverted and used up by the mundane, that your passion projects simply have nothing left to fuel them, to keep them alive.

The same entropy the that will usurp the proper functioning of your household, can potentially overtake your goals and potentially destroy them. I have often wondered what the world might be like if we all lived with enough passion and purpose to do all the things for which we are truly called.

Rather than wasting our lives in a cold, desperate attempt to avoid the hard stuff, we could be building a head of momentum towards the accomplishment of our dreams. What would it be like if we, rather than skulking about in a quiet desperation, what if we lived with passion, purpose and enthusiasm for life?

This is your life. You get one chance, and you get to choose. You get to do with it whatever you really, *really* want to do. So, decide what you want. Know that this is far more right than not doing it. I encourage you to let go of whatever is stopping you. Embrace every opportunity to foster your goals, dreams, commitments and passion.

1. What have you made a commitment to do, formally or informally, in your home, job, or life? Is it fulfilling your destiny or just filling time?

2. What goals have you set that you really want to accomplish this year? Do you own them, or do they own you?
3. Are you moving towards your goals? If not, what is stopping you from accomplishing them.

Day 2: Doing the Right Thing

I am proud of myself. Today, I seemed to get it right. I was a blur of wisdom and action, and I didn't miss a beat. Reacting and responding quickly and efficiently, I answered questions, fixed problems, and put things in order.

Urgency can definitely be a great motivator. Hit with a crisis, we don't think twice about whether we are in the right or the wrong game. We react. We move. We make things happen because we have to.

Without the urgency of crisis, it is easy to become too lax. We risk being so relaxed that we can't make anything happen. What if we could capture the urgency required to get it done, but leave behind the drama, the adrenaline, the fear, that goes along with crisis?

I believe that remembering your purpose might be just the thing to create the urgency we need. In other words, our purpose can be the necessary motivation that keeps us moving in the right direction. To stress over our exact place in time or in the universe, can definitely put too much pressure on the here and now.

Instead, I think it is wise to learn to trust that you are in the right place, and you belong. That you have actually been appointed to this thing and therefore, can then move forward with the confidence that this is the right thing for you, right now. Perhaps what you are doing is not your favorite job in the world, but it may very well be moving you toward your ultimate goal. Doing whatever you choose to do with real passion and commitment, will mean more to you and everyone around you, than doing it with half your heart.

It all starts with some firm goal setting. Take 5-10 minutes of dedicated time today and list 5 things that you really want to accomplish over the next year. Then, take an honest look at your schedule and see if where you are spending your time lines up with the goals that you have set.

Today, I encourage you to let go of the striving. Set some really big goals and don't sell yourself short. Take big steps to accomplish each item on your list. Try to embrace each of the roles. I notice that I am much happier and energized when I don't resist or resent.

Apply yourself to the process, whatever that is. Trust that this is the right thing and do it with *gusto*.

"And whatever you do, whether in word or deed, do it all in the name of the Lord Jesus, giving thanks to God the Father through Him."
--Colossians 3:17

1. Write down 5 things that you want to accomplish this year.
2. Write down 5 things that you could do, this week, that will move you towards accomplishing those things.
3. Now, write down 5 things that you could do today, to move you towards those same things.

Day 3: Do the Work...

Be strong and courageous and do the work. Do not be afraid or discouraged for the Lord God, my God, is with you. He will not fail you nor forsake you, until all the work for the service of the temple of the Lord is finished. --1 Chronicles 28:20

This was some much-needed encouragement given to King David, as he undertook the re-building of the temple of Israel. Clearly, this was a significant assignment. Our humble lives pale in comparison. And yet, I know that God cares about the details of our lives *just as deeply*. I also believe that those promises made to David all those years ago, can be applied to our lives, today.

Stop and read that again. "*He will not fail you or forsake forsake you* until **all the work** *for the service of the temple of the Lord is finished.*" Although the work is different, this promise holds for you and for me.

How many times have you cried out to God, like me, feeling utterly forsaken? Or if not completely forsaken, at least feeling like it is *all* up to you.

Try to remember that *"I am that I am"* is not about to quit. It is as though the Creator of the universe is coaxing, gently insisting, "Just do it". In that light, what would you do if you knew that you could not fail? I know, that's a big question. But seriously, what *would* you do?

Fearing that the thing we really want to do is too much, too hard, too impossible, we give up way too soon. I can easily talk myself out of things. I would rather abort the mission before I have invested too much time and effort. Somehow, in my mind, it is better to quit before I start than waste valuable time on something I might fail at. So, I quit, before I start.

"Our deepest fear is not that we are inadequate. Our deepest fear is that we are powerful beyond measure." --Nelson Mandela

We sometimes fear the hard work or who we have to become...to accomplish our goals. No matter how daunting it might be, no matter how crazy or epic the effort, God promised to be *with* us.

It can almost seems too much of a mantle to carry, just too big, too much responsibility. Confronted with something so big, we find that it is easier to back off, or back away, or simply give up...

The question never really occurred to me before I read this passage of scripture. But, what if He really did *stay* in the game on our behalf, long after we have given up? If He really did so, how would you feel, knowing that you didn't stay in there with Him?

Please know that you are not in this alone, ever, and certainly not when the going gets tough. Let's remember, that God, has infinitely more invested in us than we can imagine. And he *is* playing for keeps.

1. What would you do with your life, if you knew that you could not fail?
2. What are you *not* doing that might leave God holding up your end of the bargain?
3. What work do you need to do today to accomplish your goal?
4. In what ways, specifically, do you feel you need *divine* intervention?

Day 4: Stir Up the Spirit Within You

Today, I am writing because everything else in my life, *feels* like an obligation. I am writing in an attempt to stir up my spirit, the Spirit of God within me. That same Spirit that has seemed hauntingly quiet over the past few months. Like a parched survivor of a long drought, I have given up on rain. I am hoping for the merest sprinkle, even a mist of inspiration, something that might keep my own interest long enough to actually make it to the page.

I am not sure, really, what type of inspiration I am looking for. All I know, is that that inspiration seems to have "no business with me" right now. I talk myself out of all my best ideas and I can't bear to put my fragile heart on the line by being openly available, as I wait to be chosen by God and His inspiration. The risk of rejection seems just too high a price to pay.

Perhaps it is also the fear of failure or fear that I am incapable of capturing the essence of whatever inspiration might happen by. Or maybe the fear of inadequacy. Or maybe the fear of not being special or having important to say. These unfounded fears have me all but paralyzed, scared away from even the smallest effort.

A few years ago, I completed my first novel and I jumped right into the sequel. It seemed to serve as an elixir to my beaten-down soul after the process of editing, streamlining and publishing. Somehow, that free flow of words seemed to shelter me from the grueling work of getting the next book out there.

I whole-heartedly accepted the call to do just that and on the days that I missed, I felt I was missing everything. Not in the sense that God loved me any less, but in the very real sense that He created me for this, and I was letting Him down if I didn't, at the very least, show up.

I realized how very much I enjoyed the creative work, the actual stringing together of words, the caressing, the massaging, perfecting and then actually seeing the needle move forward on my word count. This is so unlike the cutting and pruning and chopping of word count with the editing process.

This is what my soul longs for. There is a determinedness that comes to my life when I have had the time, or made the time, to put my thoughts down on paper. There is a sense of rightness that I feel when I have been able to do some work, put something in order.

And so it is with you. What brings out the best in you? What seems to put you in order like nothing else? What makes you come away feeling like you have really done something?

1. Are you working towards your big goal every day?
2. What tends to get in the way of your work?
3. How can you push that thing aside and ensure that you show up to your actual calling every day?

Day 5: Shine Your Light

It seems a rather obvious conclusion, then, that the struggle *is* the work. Getting past the blocks, thinking it through, creating clarity and putting it down, no matter how difficult the process. This is indeed the essence of it, and I must carry on, for a part of me will surely die if I am not allowed this freedom.

I hate bad news. No, really. So much so, that avoid all news sources almost at all costs.

I still hold to the old adage: "If you can't say anything nice, don't say anything at all." Likewise then, I feel like I have no business listening to all the stuff that will bring me down. The media likes to hype us all up with all the bad in the world. Maybe they are legitimately trying to help us make sense of it all or even somehow console their listeners. While that may certainly have some benefit, I personally can't take the re-telling, the re-hashing and for that I am actually thankful. Because I can't take it, I just don't.

My other concern is that the more we see, listen and remain captivated by all this bad news, the more we risk getting too de-sensitized to recognize tragedy and grieve appropriately. We are so familiar with the bad that it begins to become commonplace and even acceptable in our lives.

This brings me back to why we cannot quit. Every time we *choose love* and not hate, we shine our light and dispel the darkness. I am so dismayed at the cloak of darkness that is pervading our world, that literally cannot standby and watch. And by not watching, I feel in some way I am shining my light in protest. I know that the two don't correlate directly, but there *is* something in me that refuses to engage, even if it is in the passive form of simply watching.

For me, it feels like it is time to engage in lighting the darkness, once and for all. And stop quitting. There is something deep within me that innately knows that I must stand up for light, *for good*, in the very face of evil. Every time I don't, I am surrendering in a small way to that presence of evil. Every time we are cavalier about the darkness, we give in to it.

1. What is your light?
2. How do you best shine your light?
3. How can you dispel the darkness in your life by shining your light?

Day 6: Standing Your Sacred Ground

Today, there was not enough of me to go around. Seriously. While I was scrambling to gather all the items needed for an off-site event tomorrow, I was interrupted at every turn. I couldn't remember what I packed or didn't and I found myself constantly misplacing my list. I literally came around a corner only to find someone else needing something.

Sometimes, it feels like there is some silent, complex plan, constantly working against me to drain the life out of me. This force is bleeding me dry of every last bit of energy. I know that sounds a bit extreme, but when your energy gets so divided, so used up, it is hard to feel like you have any force *left* to accomplish anything. Do you ever feel like that?

> *"Your enemy the devil prowls around like a roaring lion looking for someone to devour."* ---1 Peter 5:8

So it true that there actually is a force working against me. But, wait! We can take heart in the fact that Jesus, our mediator and protector, is also constantly watching and working on our behalf. When the agents of distraction are well-meaning staff members, trusting patients, and real live people in my own family, I find it to be a challenge to stay focused.

Sometimes, when I am exhausted, I have to take a step back and realize that their problem, their idea, whatever it is that needs my attention, is coming from a living, breathing human being. I catch myself in a bit of a frenzy, meeting everyone else's needs.

Distracted by each crises crisis or request, I don't realize that I am giving myself away, bit-by-bit. Soon, it seems, I feels like I am wandering around aimlessly, looking for the next person to help. And then comes the resentment. How did this happen when I pride myself in being focused and productive and accomplishing?

So, how in the world do I get back to my calling, my writing? How do I get back to the things that matter to me and call to my soul?

"I am going home." I say and head out the door. That is how. I must stand my sacred ground. Even as I do, though, I struggle with the work I left behind. An envelope that needs to be mailed. One more patient that I *should* have seen.

As I am climbing into my car, a staff member finds me. She just had "one more question". An easy one, this time, about what to wear tomorrow. I swallow my irritation. She actually cares about the event and her appearance enough to ask. I reply with a kindness that surprises me. A simple answer.

"I am sorry the other shirt didn't work." I say and I mean it. She just needed approval. The official stamp. The okay. She is a good team member, and she has my back.

I wonder, as I drive away, if that was a *test*. Maybe directly from the staff member? Or more probably from the universe. I am proud of myself, either way, because this time, I think I *passed*. The victory is short-lived and bittersweet, when I realize that I am late again for my writing time. I stayed at work too long.

Solving problems, putting out fires, over-extending myself, I find that I am often late. Never getting to some things. Rarely doing the things that I really love. Then becoming resentful, like it is somehow *their* fault.

Standing my sacred ground is what gives me the strength to make good decisions in the moment. Standing my sacred ground is what gives me the legs to stand on, when the going gets tough. If I never exercise them, I can easily fall for anything.

Right now, I am enjoying these precious moments of writing. The mantle seems to get heavier with each passing day that I don't get to it. Today, though, it feels just right. It is a therapy of sorts, and I am relieved that I am here, better late than never.

I am standing on very sacred ground and moving forward from that strength.

Remember, it is harder to knock a moving ship off her course.

1. What is your sacred ground?
2. How can standing your ground make you better able to fulfill your daily responsibilities?
3. What is one thing you can do to guard your sacred ground and/or remind yourself in the moment, that you need to stand strong?

Day 7: Live by Faith:

My perfectionism paralyzes me. Sometimes, even as I write, I delete, I edit, I butcher the very thing that I am trying so desperately to get down on paper. Other times, I convince myself that I am simply too busy to write at all. I start, I stop, I hesitate, my enthusiasm flags. And I know that I am not alone. Writers can be the *worst* in their need to be perfect. And the inevitable paralysis is a natural consequence.

It seems, though, that it may all come down to this burning desire to be *good enough*. Fear of failure, fear of judgment, fear of not getting it quite right. Self-condemnation. Self-flaggelation, even.

However, God assures us that:

"But my righteous one will live by faith. And I take no pleasure in the one who shrinks back"
--**Hebrews 10:38**

We need to get this into the deepest parts of us. We are not only forgiven, but called to hold a place of honor is in the kingdom. We dare not shrink back or wilt away from whatever it is that we are called to do. Please know that you are more than qualified, more than accepted. You are **ordained** to do the work. So, why do we tend shrink back? We may shrink away when we are feeling inadequate or disqualified, even foolish. Then we allow ourselves to think that we can't possibly live up to anyone's expectations.

Today, I found myself stuck in overwhelm. Not really knowing which way to turn or where to start. It is a sickening feeling, really. And I know that I am probably not alone. Being overwhelmed has almost become the norm, rather than the exception. But feeling overwhelmed is the thing that takes us over, leaves us disheveled, sometimes outraged, often bedraggled, and at times, undone.

For me, the only antidote to feeling overwhelmed is to take action. That is, to literally place one foot in front of the other and move forward with the next right thing. This doesn't have to mean impetuous action, but it does mean doing something, even if it is wrong.

See, the only way to get through something is to actually move through it. It is this very movement that changes us. It is the forcing ourselves to do it, the act of challenging ourselves, when we are not quite sure how it will go. The unknown, the uncertainty...this is what grows us, makes us stronger, braver, smarter.

It is okay to feel inadequate, temporarily. I think that it not only normal but healthy. It is what pushes us to get better. As long as we eventually figure out just how adequate we really are. We build adequacy muscle by staying in the game, by working through challenges. By showing ourselves that we can figure it out.

I dare you to try it. Take action today. Risk being imperfect. Risk being wrong. Move first and *then* look around. And don't forget to enjoy the journey.

1. What is one thing that you can do today, that you may have been shrinking away from?
2. Can you think of a time when you took the a risk and it paid off?
3. Think of someone you know who takes action *anyway*, despite the inherent risks or an apparent inadequacy. What can you learn vicariously from their willingness to act?

8

Steps For Tomorrow

Our future is created in the dailyness of our lives. Everyday we make choices that will impact our future. And everyday, most of us function like there is *only* today. Or, we allow our past to stop us from moving ahead in the present and consequently, our future.

I think there is a sweet spot that can be found if we take the time to really wrestle with the idea of who we are, and who we want to become. We would do well get really clear on how to spend our present so that our tomorrow is all that we hoped it would be. In this context, choosing well now will be the easiest decision we make.

While our past success can give a powerful confidence-boost, most of us allow our mistakes and the guilt and the shame that goes with them to follow us. If there was anything in the world that is able to kill your dreams faster than shame, I have yet to find it.

Our past can be a powerful spring board and I encourage you to think of it that way. You should be very familiar with all the success, all that you have learned, experienced and come through, and then use it to your advantage. By doing so, you will be better able to embrace today and live into it fully.

Your future will be created by what you choose *today*. This means who you are today matters. And who you are today, will determine who you get to become. So, let's choose wisely.

Day 1: Discipline: It is Never as Bad as it Seems.

Today, I had to make a tough phone call. I stewed about it all weekend and tried to predict all the details ahead of time. It was not the all-time most difficult call I have ever had to make, but as a result of my visualizing and even anticipating all of the worst case worst-case scenarios, I was convinced that it would be. In a desperate hope to pre-empt all of the muck, like a child afraid of the dark, I began to conjure up all sorts of monsters.

So, with much trepidation, I forced myself to enter all the numbers to patch my way through the electronic gauntlet, relieved that she didn't pick up on the first ring. When she finally did, things started out nice, smooth, all good. Way better than expected. I had half a mind to stop right there and avoid the real reason for my call. But, I soldiered on, bolstering my voice, getting to it, fully expecting the worst...None of it happened.

Not *one thing* that I laid awake worrying about manifested. The call ended far better than I could have imagined, and I was humbly reminded of God's immense and unfathomable favor. Supernatural favor that comes from simply being His child and staying in obedience. Please don't misunderstand, we should never take His favor for granted or as reason not to prepare ahead of time.

In other words, this is not license to *not* prepare for hard things. But instead, by working and preparing, we can then confidently rest in His favor. His favor doesn't have any reasonable explanation. *Favor* is God's smile. If we are walking in obedience with to Him, it is something that we can actually count on. It seems like an unfair advantage, doesn't it? It rains down in spite of us.

So, God's amazing favor is today's reason for not quitting. My hyperactive imagination created misery and drama before any of it ever happened, and I allowed myself to become miserable ahead of time.

None of what I worried about even came close to happening. Which, thankfully, is usually how it works.

Had a I not stepped out in obedience, with discipline, though, I would have never known the overwhelming grace God had planned for this situation. The truth is, I was actually surprised by His provision for me. And I am embarrassed by what that says about my level of faith.

Here is the takeaway. The Creator of the Universe is not only eager, but waiting, for a chance to intervene on my behalf. It seems as though these are the moments, the chances that heaven takes, chances that are put in motion by my obedience. By my discipline. Chances triggered by humble actions that allow His glory to peek through and maybe even reveal itself, through a broken, earthen vessel like me.

This stops me in my tracks and makes me want to fall down on my face in worship. The funny thing is that our required steps of obedience or discipline are usually pretty simple. Usually not a hard thing on our end. I think it is within our humanness to overcomplicate. But yet, even as He is busy running the the universe, I catch Him intervening *for me.* How amazing is that?

1. What step of obedience or discipline are you avoiding right now, because you fear the outcome?
2. What if God intervened for you? What would that mean to your eventual outcome?
3. Imagine that heaven is rooting for you and cheering you on. How does that change the game for you today?

Day 2 - What Else Will You do With Your Time?

We are all meant to do something. Not only that, but I think we really want to, do something, that is. Something productive, every day. It is built into our soul. A great example of this is to observe how most of us vacation. I am amazed at all the activities that are available for vacationers. These, of course, wouldn't exist if there wasn't a demand for it. When we go on vacation, our family is right there at the head of the line, packing in as many activities as we possibly can. All this, of course, jam-packed into time we have allotted for rest and rejuvenation.

The truth is none of us were really ever meant to be idle. As a consequence, some of us make an idol out of not being idle. For the sake of being busy, we pack our lives full of activity and seem powerless to stop it. Why do we do this?

It almost seems it is easier to let ourselves be pulled along by the tide of those around us, the crush of the crowd, the momentum of all the activity that surrounds us, than to set our own pace. Maybe it is FOMO (fear of missing out) or that we want a piece of the action so badly. We cannot bear the idea of being left behind.

I have realized that I may very well be shirking the important in favor of the urgent. From the outside, it appears that I have it all together and I am doing exactly what I am supposed to do. But, alas, instead, I catch myself doing far more for everyone else than I do for me. And I am guessing that I am not alone. Sometimes, I'm afraid, my sole reason is to look or feel busy.

As I write this, we are dealing with a world-wide pandemic. This has changed all of our lives in some way, for good and for bad. One of the gifts most have received, is the blessing of extra time. With events and activities being cancelled and responsibilities shifted, many of us we have newly-found margin in our schedules. For me, it has meant more time at home with my family and a significant reduction in the frenzy of life. Having nowhere to be gives me license to literally do nothing and enjoy my people.

I love the permission that last minute cancellations have afforded me. I am finding that I am working hard to hone what is really most important to me. My most significant and necessary contribution. And it definitely does not include busyness.

So, today, for the sake of my purpose and my happiness, I commit to keeping it simple. I commit to putting on my own oxygen mask before assisting others. There is great freedom in knowing that it is not all up to me. I can do this, release it, and trust that God and His perfect timing will line all the things up for His purposes.

The truth is, I can pursue the things that give me joy, especially when I am contributing to the world in a meaningful way. In fact, I think I will do it with just a bit more gusto. It is up to you and to me to choose well what we do with our time.

And that is some very good news!

1. What are you going to create today?
2. Are you staying busy for the sake of being busy sake? Allow yourself the gift of free time, taking time out of your own schedule, just for you.
3. What can you do *for you* today, for your purpose, your own nurturing, your own happiness? Make a list of all the things you love to do and begin to do them again. For you...even if it has been a long time.

Day 3 - Because it Only Takes 21 Days to Form a Habit

So, although 21 days is the general consensus, there is good research that even as little as 14 days is long enough for a repeated behavior to become a habit. It doesn't really matter how long it takes,, the process is the same. In its simplicity, if you stop doing or start doing a certain thing consistently...Voila! A new habit is formed.

Does that mean that you have to do it everyday? No. Although, sometimes that is easier. You can tailor the process to what best fits you and your lifestyle, habits can be infinitely adaptable. In fact, that is always part of what makes them stick.

The beauty of a true habit, is that if you actually form one, it fits seamlessly into your life, as though it was meant to be there. And yes, it belongs there, because it actually is there. I am not referring to self-destructive habits that we tend to habituate. I am talking about all the good things that we make consistent, like getting up at a certain time, brushing our teeth, putting our keys in a certain place. These habits tend to be self-replicating and get stronger with time, because we can see and feel the benefit of them.

It is no different with things like exercise, eating well, or self-care. I do pretty well with exercise and eating well, but deciding for me has been one of the hardest disciplines to wrangle. As I am starting to see that this can be the core of everything else that I want to accomplish, I am increasingly more motivated to do so.

I decided to *choose me* the first day I sat down to write this book. Everyday that I add a chapter, I am solidifying the habit of writing. Habits are a bit sneaky that way. They materialize mysteriously, based upon the choices we make. It is as though we wake up one day and poof...those simple, daily choices have created a brand new pattern. And that we have changed for the better.

I love that it happens this way. Try not to get caught up in all the hard work, ease into it and see what happens.

A nun's *habit* is her clothing...yes, same word. She wears this specialized headgear as a daily reminder that she is set apart for a divine purpose, given over to the service of God. Forsaking all else, she is committed sacrificing her life for that service.

Likewise, my habits dictate *who I am*. I cannot possibly have better, more focused habits unless I choose wisely the activities that I engage in. And while these habits seem to materialize out of nothing, *seemingly* out of thin air, they are, in fact, very hard won. Just like the nuns consecrate their lives, we create our habits by forsaking other choices, damping down the competing voices.

Anne Dilliard says, "How we spend our days, is indeed, how we spend our lives." So simple, so profound, so instructive.

In writing this book, I have chosen to make writing a habit. It is a habit that keeps me sane, a habit that I choose daily in the face of all the many suitors for my time. Those suitors are sometimes selfish beasts of things that will usurp my time, shamelessly stealing me away from the essence of who I am. Although they often appear harmless, noble even, they can never get enough of me. So it is with you. We must stand strong against their demands.

By choosing your cause, your mission, your creative work today, you will simply have to push back all those things that threaten to distract you, steal your essence and demand your energy. Don't be discouraged if you aren't perfect at this. Embrace the growth and development of the habit, as it is birthed, then toddles, becomes lanky and awkward, and then eventually comes into its own. It might be more than a little messy and less than perfect as it grows up.

Let's put on our new habit today as a reminder of who we are. And maybe more importantly, who we want to be. The world is ready and waiting. Your legacy is waiting. But most importantly, those habits are literally dying for a new life.

1. What habit do you want to foster over the next 21 days?
2. What step will move you closer to actually making that happen?

3. How will developing this habit bring you closer to the real you?

Day 4 - The Joy of Obedience

The joy of obedience? As we discussed earlier, no one likes being told what to do. We forget that the discipline of obedience *is* the backbone of accomplishment. Or maybe we don't make the connection at all. When I am supposed to do something, I find myself resisting at my very core. I tend to resist even harder especially if I feel like I am being bossed.

I am writing during my lunch hour today. This is often the only time I have, so I am managing to squeeze it in. Why? Mostly because I have to. Obeying in the moment, because I may not get another one. I don't have time to argue or procrastinate. It is now or never.

I cannot bear the thought of never, so now it is. Are there other things I could be doing? Absolutely. And far easier, less taxing things at that. Why not write a chapter, why not fill the time, and fill my heart at the same time? Obedience. How else do we get anything done, without the choice to obey right now. Obey the schedule. Obey. Obey. Obey. But even as I do it, I need some convincing.

My biggest enemy is a chronic lack of confidence. I find myself questioning whether or not I have anything worthwhile to say. It is so daunting to think that I might be called to contribute to someone else's well-being, that I catch myself shying away. I know I must persevere, regardless. For the discipline, for all that this does for me.

My goal: to enhance, to inspire, to bring joy. I simply can''t imagine going through life and not sharing what I have learned, particularly all the those hard-won lessons. And to that end, I catch myself openly sharing, sometimes bowling an innocent bystander completely over, with my unabridged versions of *self-helpery*. Seems, I can't help myself.

People, I'm told, don't really want the truth, but instead a whitewashed version of it. A sanitized story that is far easier to take in. The deer-in-headlights reaction confirms this. Friends, even family, aren't really prepared for the rawness of it, the ridiculousness of some of my foibles when I over-share.

When I write, I am a better person. More coherent and functional in public. Here, on the page, I am able to clearly express my truth, process it, and get it out of my head. Here, I can see it in black and white, sort it out and sometimes even be done with it. I can be clear, weed out the superfluous, stick to the essentials. I know that I am not alone. This is why self-deprecating humor is so effective and so utterly hilarious, because we have all been there. We all have our own brand of nonsense.

I have to ask the pre-eminent question then. Why else does God have us go through the pain of learning, if not to share our lessons? Maybe it feels to you, like it is too much to take on. Or maybe, like me, you think that everybody around you knows all these things already. The more I talk to people around me, though, the more I realize that they are struggling too.

Here is where obedience comes into play. For me, this means being so tuned into what God has for me *to do* today, that I can't possibly miss it. And then, simply *doing* it. Really. It is that simple. I have come to believe that every time I converse or consult or merely even speak to another human, it may very well be by divine appointment. So then, our job, in the moment, is to do the right thing. Then in the next, to do it again.

Again and again and then again, doing those simple things that we have been called to do. Obedience. Rather than living in fear of doing the wrong thing or doing the right thing in the wrong way. Simply obey...

You know the way, now walk in it. One foot in front of the other, with joy and peace...obey. And see what happens. Even better, forget completely what you just did, because it is over and done with.

Here is the thing. Without action, nothing happens. Our very existence predicates action. I am convinced that when we walk in surrendered obedience, we will be delighted to see how much we can accomplish.

"It is by acts and not by ideas that people live." --Anatole

Just one day and one step at a time. You got this. Enjoy the journey.

1. What is one thing that you know you have been called to do, but you have yet to do?
2. Do it today.
3. Schedule it into your day for tomorrow.

Day 5 - Every Step Forward is...a Step Forward!

I refuse to accept this nonsense about 2 steps forward, 3 steps back as a reason to quit. Anytime we go hard after any goal, it is to be expected that we will have disappointments, frustrations and setbacks along the way. It has been said that if you aren't disappointing yourself or failing, you may not be trying hard enough. I have disappointed myself countless times in my mundane busyness, my refusal to get down to it, and my general lack of confidence about this work.

It does feel really good to get words down on paper, to actually get something done. Somehow the victory is sweeter, when I have put off the work so many times before. It is a hard-won victory to have pushed through a very heavy curtain, or a roadblock or a fog. And when I get to the other side, I surprise myself with the relative ease of it. The words flow, the analysis is clear, and I can actually make my way.

This kind of victory is impossible if I refuse to try, of course, as I have discovered so many times in the past. At the core of the victory, is the willingness to try. This requires embracing the distinct possibility of failure. There is no such thing as failure, of course, only learning.

I'm not sure I fear failure as much as attrition. The idea of attrition or the slow slide into oblivion, forces me to come face-to-face with the reality that no one cares if I carry on or quit altogether. That possibility is far more painful to me, than simply writing something.

So, my encouragement for today, is just keep going. Like plodding up a grueling mountain, or even a very beautiful one, placing one foot in front of the other, every step really does count. Every step is making bits of progress in the right direction. Always.

1. Review the progress you have made in a particular area. Don't judge, just be brutally honest. Even the ugly and painful can mean you are moving forward.

2. Journal about your progress, give yourself a pat on the back and keep going.
3. Do it again. Move forward, that is, and don't forget to have some fun along the way.

Day 6 - Here I am, Send Me!

"Then I hear the voice of the Lord saying, "Whom shall I send? And who will go for us?
And I said, "Here am I. Send me!" --Isaiah 6:8

So, I had a conversation with a friend yesterday who confessed with brutal honesty, that even as a Christian, he doesn't think he does one thing a day that pleases God. That is, for the sole purpose of pleasing God. Admittedly, he further confessed, his prayer and devotional time may qualify, but beyond that, he thought, everything else he did, had another self-serving purpose.

I challenged and encouraged him with the example of his work, which is how he spends the majority of his time. Work is something that he is very committed to, almost obsessed with. He swore that it was all for the purpose of feeding his family. When I countered, "But I think *that* is very glorifying to God." He didn't agree.

This conversation made me re-think my own desire to please God through my everyday activities. I don't think I am called to full-time ministry. Not only do I not have the proper education or credentials, I also don't think I have it in me to do that work.

As a firm believer in the promise that God will, in fact, grant the desires of my heart, as I seek to follow Him, daily...I know that there is something here on the page for me to do.

"Take delight in the Lord, and he will give you the desires of your heart."
--Psalm 37:4

For there is nothing in the world that my heart desires more than this. Stringing words together on the page, honoring God, and speaking openly about may my faith and hope in Christ. There is nothing that I would rather do than this.

And yet, like this frighteningly honest confession, I am not that different than my friend. I find myself doing many things other than this. Things that appear to be urgent. Self-serving things that draw my attention and my energy away and ultimately keep me away from this.

Even as I write, today, I ask myself 'why'. Why is it so easy toI allow things to take my attention away, why am I so easily distracted?. Why is this so very hard to get to? It seems that I have conditioned myself for the *urgent*. Perhaps it is answering the adrenaline rush that goes along with the momentary stress of each day, or the fact that "real work" seems so much more tangible. But the truth remains, this work that I am doing with you, just feels right, so much like play, that it couldn't *possibly* be valuable for anything!

This is the *desire of my heart*. I have loved books for as long as I can remember and it is through words on a page that I have learned how to love God. It is here that I find my purpose, if for no other reason, I write to point my reader to the Savior, who gave His all for us. That we might have eternal life and an abundant life in the here and now. It is the least I can do, offering the gift of my words, my time, my life, the *author* and finisher of my faith.

The joy that comes back to me is immeasurable. I love how I feel when I have penned my thoughts and know that somewhere out there, there might be someone who will be encouraged, who might take my musings to heart, who might also figure out what they were put on this earth to do and then begin to do it.

1. What are you doing right now that gives you real joy, that could be the desire of your heart?
2. Could you give yourself permission to do that thing? When?
3. Think of the ways your joy could be glorifying to God or how your thing might bring someone else true joy.

Day 7 - Leave No Arrows in My Quiver

Billy Graham died today. At the age of 99, he passed, peacefully, we are told, to a literal out-of-this-world reward. The radio station played "Come to the Table", in tribute, as they announced the news, and I teared up, picturing Reverend Graham joyfully greeted by all the souls whom he had influenced during his earthly ministry. I pictured multitudes lining up to thank him for fearlessly sharing the gospel, so that they too might come to the table.

One of the true greats, honored by Christians and non-Christians the world over, he was the real deal: trustworthy, articulate, powerful yet humble. He made more of an impact on twentieth century Christianity than any other person in my lifetime. I want to stop everything right now to honor his memory. But at the same time, I am super-motivated to pick up my pen and write. Yes, I need to write, something, anything, that might be influential to the kingdom. Oh God, might I be a voice for you in the impending silence? And if not me, then who?

Even if I started right now, I don't have a chance of living up to his legacy. My heart *aches* for the silence, the void that is left in his absence. Reverend Billy Graham has earned his heavenly rest and he will be missed beyond measure. In spite of the fact that there was no one quite like him and will never be another to replace him, I know that the Creator of the universe isn't surprised or the least bit worried now, for He is constantly working in the background. Raising you and I up to do our work, on the heels of such a legacy. All the more reason for each of us to courageously speak His truth, boldly, vigorously, according to our individual passions and callings.

I encourage you not to shrink away, but instead to embrace the opportunity laid before you. God was and is and forever *will be* waiting for you to take it on and continue the legacy. He is right there in the wings waiting to empower you. All we need to do is ask. To rise up and do our work. The world is waiting to hear from you. Today, more than ever before…

1. Do you have a story or truth that is uniquely yours, that needs a voice?
2. Think deeply about the most effective way to share it.
3. What would motivate you, right now, to give your story away? The world is waiting. And ready. You are right on time.

9

Gut Check: Getting Super Honest

We have covered a great deal of ground together and I love that you are still here. Personally, I often ditch my best ideas and even almost finished projects at this stage, when I am getting close to the end, when I am all but *at* the finish line..

Having caught myself in the act of quitting so many times before, I am onto myself. Right now, I am feeling a bit like there is nothing else to say. I am wondering if you have enjoyed this or learned anything. And yet, it seems, I have so much more to say.

This chapter is all about asking even harder questions with the hope that you will be brutally honest with yourself. If you are still thinking about quitting, I hope that this gut-level honesty will keep you in the game.

As you level with yourself, I hope that your self-nurture and your knowledge of yourself will thrive and then motivate you to take those big important steps.

Regardless, as you go deeper, I really hope that you will discover who you are and what you really want to do with yourself, with no need to prove yourself or hide from discovery.

I'm right here with you. Let's go.

Day 1: What if No One Gives Back?

Confession time. While I pride myself on being a generally helpful and a pretty good person, I find myself often looking for, at the very least, *a thank you*. I can't seem to help it. I am disappointed when no one notices. My husband doesn't re-pay me in kind and no one buys *my* Starbucks' drive-thru, though I often treat the car behind me.

Or even worse, my kindness somehow backfires. Knowing the discomfort of being new in a group, I tend to be the one who reaches out to make any newcomer feel welcome. I catch myself offering unsolicited help, which comes very naturally to me. It is not unusual for the object of my assistance a bit put off with my efforts. They are surprised and often hesitant to accept my grace, but those are *i*nherent risks we take if we truly offer ourselves in self-sacrifice and strive to die to ourselves.

Is this how Jesus felt when he came to seek and save the lost? When we spat in his face and flat-out rejected him? And that was the most pious among us. The Pharisees and Saduccees, who were actually the most vocal and the most violent. I know my bits of small assistance hardly compare, but still.

I sometimes wonder if He would have simply stayed safe had He known that His kindness would be met with such utter irreverence. Then, I remember, that He *did* know. Before the foundations of the world, He knew.

Makes us re-think our smatterings of goodwill, doesn't it? How did He stay in the game, knowing the eventual outcome? He said He only does what he sees His Father doing. In other words, not His will, but Thine be done.

Likewise, for us, then. It's pretty simple, really. What we do for others should never be *for us*, but for *them*. And more accurately *for Him*. All our goodness as His hands, His feet. Jesus with skin on. When I think about Jesus and His earthly ministry, I get the feeling that He never needed reimbursement. He didn't earn anything. Sure, He had crowds that followed Him, but none of what He did was for paybacks. Oh, that I could imitate that.

Today, I encourage you to do what you do because no one will pay you back. We have only one chance and our lives are so very short.

1. What can you do today for someone in your life that may never be reciprocated or rewarded?
2. Has it held you back, at times, when nobody notices your service?
3. What would Jesus do?

Day 2: In Sickness and In Health

I have been under the weather lately. Well, as much as I hate to admit it, I have been sick. Really sick. See, I don't like to admit this, because I'm a doctor, and *if* I am a good doctor or a smart doctor, I should never get sick. It feels like weakness. It feels like I have failed or done something very wrong.

My logical brain knows better. The truth is, I have been stressed out, run down, and pushing too hard. Maybe because I wasn't stopping, my body stopped me. Because, I *am* a good and smart doctor, I recognize this.

So, as I make my way back to health, I am careful to ease back in. I am writing. Writing to right myself. To get my sea legs under me, to put things right. It feels therapeutic, as though I am massaging my tired soul, bit by tiny bit, back into the real world. Emerging one word at a time, ever so softly, treading carefully, so as not to jar my wearied bones. Or to set myself back.

I find it interesting that this is often the first place I come, to my writing, as my point of re-entry. Ironically, I don't have the same trepidation that I do on a normal, healthy day. Because I have been sick, this work feels like a bonus. Therefore, regardless of how anyone might evaluate it, *I am impressed*. This *is* an impressive feat, to ease back into my work and onto my feet.

I realize three important things. First, how very much I cherish this work, that I will return to it the minute I am able or like right now, even before I am fully able. I am proving my commitment to myself, in sickness and in health.

Secondly, this work is noteworthy, and I shouldn't have to be sick to merit my own recognition. Today, for some reason, I don't need to wait for the acclaim of anyone. It feels good and healthy to recognize myself for what I am doing here.

Thirdly, I can't help but see the how I take my healthy life for granted, the boundless energy that I have been blessed with when I am firing on all cylinders. How true it is that life is short. Too short, to accomplish every single thing we would like to do. We must budget our time, our resources, our life force, our days.

As you pursue your passion project today, I encourage you to remember your own commitment. *In sickness and in health*. I hope you can recognize how important, how significant your work is. And I hope you don't have to get sick to see it.

1. Is there one thing that you would love to spend more time on?

2. Are you running yourself ragged, pursuing other things?

3. Make the switch today. Life is way too short to waste your precious time.

Schedule the time and actually *do* it. Today.

Day 3 - I Feel like I am Forgetting Something

As I struggle with balancing my day job, my home life, and this writing project, I am at the mercy of my limited energy and failing memory. Juggling all responsibilities, remembering all the minutiae, keeping myself on track, is all at the mercy of my own sometimes fallable mind.

Much to my chagrin, it is not a fool-proof system. Though I try really hard not to, I do forget stuff. As a result, I have this almost constant feeling of impending doom. The feeling that I have forgotten something vital, something that I should have done yesterday, or last week or even last month. And no, I don't think it is clinical anxiety, although it seems to masquerade like it

It really is more than a bit crazy, though, and full-on nonsense. In reality, I am actually successfully accomplishing more than I give myself credit for. As I struggle to be independent, I rarely ask for help, always try to make my own way and work hard not to impose. Still, I am human, and I do forget things. And I am way too hard on myself when I do.

It comes down to getting a handle on *the important* versus *the urgent*. Stephen Covey was one of the first to address this revolutionary idea in his classic work, The 7 Habits of Highly Effective People. His contention was that when we routinely allow the *urgent* to usurp the *important,* we burn-out, victories feel empty, and we ultimately lose track of our fundamental purpose.

Today, I have chosen well. I have taken time to write first. I love when I choose it first, because, at least for today, I will not get my priorities jumbled and inadvertently miss my mark. I love when I choose well, because, at least for right now, there is no pressure. It just feels right and nurturing and constructive.

I know that I am not alone in the struggle against allowing the urgent to surpass the important. So, I am certainly not here to judge.

But, we must understand, if we do it enough, the important will have fallen off your radar in favor of the urgent. The important will no longer have any pull or hold or any real significance for you. Soon, the important may pass you over completely, while someone else picks up your ball and runs with it.

See, if the words that God lays on our hearts are important enough for us, then surely the words that we leave unsaid and unwritten very well could be picked up by another.

So, let's get to it today. Do the most important thing first and let the chips fall where they may. Perhaps what we are deeming urgent might need to find another owner, so that our *important* can get done today. And that someone might be more passionate and even more capable at our *urgent* thing. Let's get to work.

1. What is your first priority today?
2. How can you choose your *important*, before the urgent?
3. Schedule that thing in, right now, so that you don't miss out on it, for another day.

Now, breathe. You are home. And it's okay, you deserve to *love* what you do.

Day 4 - Why Not?

What is it that you are *most* passionate about? And I mean really passionate. I have observed the strangest combinations of passions in people. My husband is full-time chiropractor, who is crazy-devoted to his work. He is also passionate about moto-crossing, playing the banjo, triathloning, his family, and chocolate chip cookies.

How do I know this? Well, he organizes his spare time around all these sacred things. I, in stark contrast, find myself short-changing my hobbies, for the service of others. He may not utter it along aloud, but anytime he has a free moment, off he goes, in the direction of this hobby or that. Sometimes, it just has to be that simple.

There is something to be learned from that. I really wish I was more that way. Instead, I over-complicate, over-think, over-analyze. And with my over-analysis goes any chance that I will actually do something about it. Paralysis by analysis.

While hubby's motto seems to be, "just do it", mine might be more like, "just think about it"! In my defense, I don't actually do nothing but sit and think, I keep myself in pretty constant motion. And generally producing something significant, along the way.

The trouble is, I am rarely at play. In fact, it might be this chronic lack of play that creates a bit of a grind from day-to-day! If I didn't love my work, I wouldn't be so steeped in it, so caught up, so distracted.

What I don't love is that I never have time, or make time, for play. So that is my pledge for today. By whispering the words, "Why not?" I am going to remind myself of the importance of enjoying life, amidst the work. Setting my face like flint towards my goals, and going about all my work with a delighted smile, knowing that the fun is just around the corner, or maybe even built into the very thing I am doing, right now. Why not?

1. Name 3 healthy, nurturing things that you can do regularly just for the *fun* of it.
2. Schedule time to do those things.
3. Now actually go & and do them and have some fun! I promise you will be more productive with the important things, having had some quality self-nurture time.

Chapter 5 - Quit Being Distracted!

I actually had some time to write, today. I had a few precious hours with nothing to do. Okay, well, not really nothing, but nothing more pressing. No appointments, no deadlines, nothing that had to be done. Actual free time. So rather than sitting down to it, I needlessly micromanaged my mom's painting of a room. I ordered some birthday gifts and snacked my way through several hours.

Ironically, I was well-aware that the seconds, the minutes, and then the hours were slipping through my grasp. Free time flying away, frittering off like a butterfly, giving me the sense that it was still very much there in its entirety, even while it was vanishing in plain sight. After all, free time is in fact free. When I finally pulled myself away from the painting and the snacks, I realized that I wasn't hungry at all and the room was taking shape completely without me. Quicker even, if I didn't hover.

When I eventually sat down to it, I realized to my absolute joy and relief, that this project has a life of its own. It wants to get written as much as I want to write it. The words flow effortlessly now. Is it *because* I have procrastinated and that the words are ripe unto harvest? Perhaps readied by all the pent up, mute polishing that has gone on far too long inside my head, I am now ready to write.

So, once again I have to facee the question: why do I let myself become distracted? Shying away from what I desperately want and need to accomplish? Today, I will have to boil it down to its foundation, which is probably steeped in fear and not faith. Fear that the newly painted room won't be to my liking, Fear that I will starve to death without that snack. Fear that this project isn't a viable thing at all. That one, of course, being the most paralyzing of them all. Even though all those other things seem so much more real and tangible.

Sitting down to work, though, I am delighted to see that the words on the page are answering back with a sort of resonance that makes all of this worth it. Instead of being an ethereal, figment of my imagination, this happy place turns out to be every bit as real as the newly painted room.

Tomorrow, I will remind myself of the painful process I have inflicted on myself once again. I must remind myself of the ridiculousness of my own ridiculousness and just get down to it. Once again, the page will await my arrival, patiently biding its time. Always there, always at the ready, and always available, always ready.

Perhaps my real folly is that I often forget that *I too* need to be ready. My job is to wait patiently for inspiration, to hear the whispers of God to my heart. Perhaps, I need to view *my role* as the lady-in-waiting, always at the ready. And then to get to it, when these open spans of time occur, when the previously unseen opportunities present themselves.

As I wrap up this chapter, I am reminded that my time is not unlimited. It is time for dinner and I need to get out for a run. So, to think that I have an oasis of free time is profoundly false. Yet another reason to get down to the work when we can. There is a sweetness that comes from *staying in the game,* being consistent in the application of your craft. Doing the practice daily, because, deep down, you really want to. It will move the needle forward, even if only by small bits and even if only eventually. Some days more than others, but always forward motion, however small the steps.

Just for today, I challenge you to stop getting distracted and get to it!

1. What inspiration do you need to motivate you to perform your best service?
2. Are you doing things that fill your time, but not your *soul?*
3. Try to remember a time when you waited for divine guidance and then proceeded with inspiration at your back.
4. Journal about your experience. How can that apply to your creative work right now?

Day 6 - Blindsided by a False Accusation

Well, today I woke up as any other day and I was getting ready to go to the office, I get a text that sent me reeling. Funny thing was, I couldn't stop or even take a break from the activity of the day to process, think, or get my wits about me. Instead, I was forced to process as I went about my business, literally going through the motions, amidst a mental and emotional storm.

In the briefest moments we had together before he left for work, my husband and I put together the details of the day and re-affirmed our love and support of one another. Solidarity, at least there was that.

The very next text I received was from a long-time friend, who, by her very presence, can bring a smile to my face. She is beautiful inside and out, and invariably has something encouraging to say even in the midst of her own personal storms. Not surprisingly, her encouragement was exactly what I needed to hear, although she had no foreknowledge whatsoever about what was going on with me.

But isn't that how God works?

"Do not forsake the works of your hands." Psalm 138: 8

When I read the remainder of her text, packed full of scripture, I knew that this was *indeed* from the Lord, encouraging me to get on with the battle of the day. For He has already gone before, and the victory is already His. Our job is to keep moving forward, to not give up and to definitely not give in. So, in the fleeting moments I have today, I will write, because it is *right*. If I allow these random attacks to bring it all to a halt, they have won, I have surrendered.

Oh, God, give me strength to forge ahead. The words of her timely text enfolded my aching heart like a balm.

Yes, this is why I will not give up, because it is right. *It is the work of my hands*. I will not be loved by or approved of by everyone. But truly, none of that matters when I am doing this for an audience of One. None of that matters when I have nothing to prove. None of that matters because the accusers did not choose this work for me or deem me able. God did.

I have every right to move past their judgments, not spitefully, but in spite of the hurt and all their accusing. That simply is not anything that I can waste time worrying about. I will redeem my time here on earth, for it is the only chance I have to "do the works of my hands" and not forsake my calling.

1. Not everyone loves you and that's okay. Do your thing anyway and do it with gusto.
2. What are you doing to please everyone else that is not pleasing you?
3. What decisions do you need to make today that will allow you to plow through your obstacles?

Day 7 - Life is Not a Spectator Sport

I have never been much of a sports fan. I do like sports. I like the idea of them, the competition, camaraderie and even the spectating aspect. I just have a hard time being still long enough to actually watch. This is an Olympic year and while I have the utmost respect for the dedication and commitment of those athletes, I still don't find myself devoting much time to watching. I kind of admire the stamina required to spectate, I guess I am just more given to being in the game, as opposed to being on the sidelines.

One of the reasons the Olympic games are so popular is that all of us have at least a bit of desire to perform something, *anything*, on that level. There is a part of us that lives vicariously through those athletes. This is what makes those tear-jerking backstories so *tear jerking*. We see our heroes as real people, flawed, troubled. And overcoming obstacles as humans, not that different from you and me. So, if not that different, why couldn't we throw on some workout gear and join in the fray? Obviously, there is a little more to it than that...

...It is infinitely easier to sit and watch from the sidelines. Infinitely safer to criticize a play or join in a victory chant than produce your very own play, isn't it? I think this is one of the reasons that spectator sports are so popular. I think it is one of the reasons that we convince ourselves that being a spectator in life is kind of okay, too.

While it more comfortable and certainly easier to sit back and spectate, I want to remind you that your life is not a spectator sport, and if it is not a spectator sport, then nobody is watching you. Nobody cares, really, because they are too wrapped up in their own drama.

Furthermore, if they do care or take the time to watch your life, at the very least, you should give them something worth watching! We are often so worried about what others might think, that it can paralyze us. It literally stops us in our tracks. Being so wrapped up in getting everything perfect, we do nothing at all. And yes. I do speak from experience.

So, if it is perfectionism that is stopping you, let me repeat...nobody really cares. No one. They are too busy worrying about their own stuff. Life is decidedly not a spectator sport. And I do mean decidedly.

You get to decide. This is your life. This is your game. So, jump in with both feet, with your entire being. No one gets to the Olympics by being half- hearted. And that, my friend, is the real reason that we watch...

1. What is it that you know you should be doing? Have you stopped yourself because you don't think you can do it? Why or why not?
2. No one really knows how the game will go until it is played. How might your readiness develop even as you play the game?
3. What is one step that you can take right now, whole-heartedly, that might move you in the direction of your dreams?

Jump in. This is your time.

10

Setting Goals

The best set goals, the ones that we are most inclined to achieve, are those that fit conveniently into our lives. I suppose it can work, but goals that are at odds with our lifestyle, create a harder road. I'm not saying that the follow through will be easy or effortless, but the the less friction we have to getting the work done, the better.

If we can pack the practice or the subgoals neatly into our daily life with minimal disruption of our daily routines, chances are greater that we will *stick* with the game plan. Coupling those good habits with *other* good habits makes all the good things infinitely more doable.

This is why I encourage you to set goals in several different areas at once. Not to overwhelm, but instead, to give you a framework to make it all work. It actually makes sense to have a work goal, a fitness goal, family goals, and spiritual goals that you are working on...and yes, all at the same time.

That doesn't mean that you have to go hard after all of them at the same time. You may have to prioritize, shift up and down as you go along, but juggling all of the stuff may be part of the fun. And the balancing act may keep you in balance.

Day 1 - What is This All About Anyway?

Even as I catch myself being distracted by some other urgency, I wonder *why*. Why do I give in so easily? Part of it, to my credit, is that I genuinely love people and want the best for them. I want to support the people I care about in any way that I can. And so, I bend over backwards with my efforts to help. When I am truly honest with myself, though, I have to examine what I might be avoiding, dodging, refusing to face head on. Could it be that it is less risky emotionally to invest in their goals than it is to invest in my own?

Whoa. Now, that is an interesting take. And one that I must face. I must look at how important it is to invest in my own interests for the sake of my own happiness. Now we are getting somewhere. This allows me to be better equipped to handle everything that comes my way, whether it be my very own real estate or someone else's.

As I write this, I have the presence of mind to ask: Am I really helping them? Or am I merely enabling them to be more dependent on me and the help? These are incredibly important questions to ask.

It is very interesting to see what my kids, and even my husband, can accomplish when I take a step back and let them shine. This brand of tough love can be tough for both the giver and the receiver. And infinitely healthier for everyone.

Today, I want to view my life as the true vessel that I am. And I want to see what I might accomplish for God, to be His hands and feet personified. If I want to help anyone accomplish anything, it would be Him. Today, I want to do what He would be pleased to catch me doing. How about you?

1. What have you done today that you would be proud to be caught doing?
2. Is there anything that you need to stop doing?

3. How can you daily remind yourself that the essence of who you are is depending on your willingness to invest in you?

Day 2 - Staying in Gratitude

It is a wonderful day to write. But, then again, it always is. I am excited today, that I have been able to carve out a few minutes to get it done. This bit of spare time feels like a precious gift. In spite of this being a crazy, hectic week, I have been able to set boundaries and make some choices that allowed for breaks that seemed serendipitous and scrumptious, particularly because of how hectic it's been. My writing feels like an oasis. My happy place. Peaceful and lovely.

I am grateful that the hectic reflects my commitment to my family. I had to discipline my son today and while it wasn't fun for either one of us, it will make him better. Makes me a better mom. Boundaries will teach him how to behave in the future, in our family and in the world. I am grateful for that hard. It makes me stronger.

I have noticed that it is impossible to be truly grateful and angry at the same time. This might be the thing that keeps me from reacting or being locked in a negative funk. I don't have to live in that space. I can rise above, because my boundaries give me the framework to live loved and free.

Today, I am grateful for the messiness and rigors of life. It is 'the hard' that makes 'the easy' so much more enjoyable. Hard work makes rest and relaxation something to look forward to. God gives me 'the hard' to make me better, stronger, and to draw me closer to Him. Without the pressure of the hard, I become soft and often forget how much I need Him.

As I work through the hard stuff, I get stronger and more able to handle the next hard thing, so that He might be glorified through it all. And so it is for you. Stay in gratitude.

1. What are you thankful for?
2. How does gratitude motivate you?

3. Is there hard stuff in your life that you can begin to be grateful for? How is this hard stuff training you to be better?

Day 3 - As a Man Thinketh...

I have an assignment for you, today. I want to offer that you need to believe harder in yourself. No one can do this for you. Whatever you believe about yourself is true...that is, will all come true. Good or bad, you will manifest what you truly believe. If you think that you are a schmuck who will never amount to anything and you don't rise above that thinking, you will end up exactly that. If you think, in contrast, that you are a superstar, who will only be successful, eventually, at everything you do...Guess what? Your brain, your emotions, and your very actions will line up with that belief. You will somehow figure out a way to make it happen.

Here is the assignment. For the next 30 days, I challenge you to wake up every morning and visualize success in everything you do. Imagine yourself at the top of you game. Imagine yourself 20 pounds lighter. Get a picture of yourself in your finest hour and place it somewhere prominent. Look at it often. Imagine yourself calmly strolling through your day, successful, unstressed, emanating love and peace to your family.

Don't allow negative thoughts to creep into the this vision of yourself. Not for a minute. It is actually your job to stop the negative thoughts or replace them with all the thoughts you want to think on purpose. I know that you can do this.

For years, I personally looked to other people for recognition, as a sort of third-party endorsement. This was the only way I could really be assured that what I was doing was right or okay or acceptable. And, of course, for years, I have failed to ever really feel endorsed at all.

I have since learned that I am way more effective when I wholeheartedly accept who I am, right now. Not when this or that goal is met, not when this or that improvement is done. Right now.

So go ahead and love yourself. Love yourself unconditionally. Love yourself with abandon. For all your quirks and for all your foibles. Begin to take joy in your journey and laugh a little more.

My hope is that all your good vibes will spill over into every aspect of your life and then onto the people that you rub shoulders with. Refuse to get caught up in their nonsense or their unbelief, but instead, sprinkle bits of happiness onto them. Remember it is none of your business what anyone thinks of you. *None* of your business.

Your business is to create all joy and peace and love that you can. And by doing so, you will make everyone else around you a bit happier. You will become magnetic, I promise.

1. Do you have a clear picture of yourself as you truly want to be?
2. Take some time and really brainstorm this. Get very detailed, make it real.
3. What if you could do anything in the world, no limits, what would it be?

Day 4 - Sitting

I was remembering a playdate a few years ago. Jonnie had waited all summer. He had been begging me to text the mom, he missed his buddy and, in his defense, was tired of "hangin' with the girls". All great reasons for a playdate, and to top it off, everything went so smoothly. The boys were obedient, there was no trouble with the younger brother who fearlessly tagged along, and Jonnie was the perfect little host.

The other mom and I hit it off, had a nice chat, there was no trouble disengaging at the end, and I made it to work in time for my afternoon shift. Neat, tidy, perfect. Right? While this seemed like the perfect way to wile away a few hours, I realized in retrospect that I sat for too long, ate things that I don't normally eat, didn't make any progress on my writing, and gained 2 two pounds overnight.

I know it was right for Jonnie. And, arguably, I needed the time away from constant work and yes, the weight gain was probably from the fast food, since I didn't have time to pre-prepare something healthy amidst all my lounging.

I could have definitely thrown something in the crockpot, since I was home the whole time and it would have been completely appropriate to monitor that as we chatted. I could have suggested a walk, she would have probably been game. But I didn't and now I am left with the guilt over having 'done it wrong'. The truth is: What's done is done and I can't go back, so there is little benefit to over-analyzing. However, had I chosen for me and advocated for my own needs in the moment, though, I think this could have been had a much better outcome for me and the other mom. Without losing a bit of fun or frolicking for the kids.

Today, I encourage you think about what you need *right now*. This doesn't have to mean that you do that thing at the expense of the other people in your life. Likewise, you don't have to neglect *you* when you choose for them! You really can choose you **and** *choose them*. In fact, I think that is the healthiest way to do it.

I am writing now because it nurtures *me*. I am writing with my whole heart because it affords a sort of specialized rest, restoration and recreation that doesn't exist anywhere else in my life. And yes, I do mean *recreation*. Actually re-creation. Taking all of my world experiences and re-creating them on the page to make sense, to learn, to grow and then to share.

True recreation can bring a sense of accomplishment. It allows us the luxury of relaxation, but gives that irreplaceable 'ahhh' feeling that we have done some very good work. Like a good run, painting or gardening, there is an inherent reinforcement of our innate creative side. Creator God within us.

This is why we all long to *make* and *do*. While idleness may seem easier in the moment, if we make it an idol, we will discover what a cruel taskmaster it is. It will rob us not only of our income, the cleanliness and order of our homes, but more importantly, our purpose, our self-worth and perhaps the manifestation of the glory of God within us.

See, to truly manifest God within us, I think we have to get moving, keep creating, start doing. While not frenzied, I am certain that the same God who sustains the universe, doesn't idle away time.

Coming full circle, I am eager to jump back into life today and to do it with gusto. So thankful that I have productive, much-needed work to do and that without my work, the world may not be quite as orderly, quite as well put together and ultimately not as well-adjusted.

I know the same is true for you. Go and do likewise.

1. What is one thing that you can do today that serves as re-creation for you and possibly the world?
2. What stops you from digging in and doing it?
3. Do you catch yourself whiling away hours in *default* activities? Are you following the path of least resistance or purposefully moving forward?

Day 5 - Ten Years From Now

I just received an email from me. It was an assignment that I was given a year ago at a coaching intensive, that is, to write a letter to myself *from myself* in 10 years. The aim was to picture myself in the future with as much detail as possible and write from that place.

I remembered do this assignment very well. I drew a complete blank. I had nothing. It seems that I had no long-term goals. I had apparently drifted into a sort of gridlock, stuck in survival-mode and as part of that survival, turned off anything that was not urgent. The demands of the day were so overwhelming, that I couldn't let myself think of another thing. I wasn't thinking or planning past today.

How could I possibly have gotten to this point? And more importantly, not even be aware of it? I have always been a planner and a goal-setter. Worse than that, I realized that I really had forgotten the reasons I was doing many of the things. My goals had turned into short-term, moment-by-moment to-do lists. No wonder I felt like I was floating along aimlessly.

As I forced myself to think about ten years from now, I saw that I had to get clear on the things that I wanted to do and who I wanted to be. I needed to clarify my purpose. I really wondered how I had allowed myself to get so caught up in the day-to-day. Was I using the busyness of the present moment to escape the hard work of my heart's most precious desire?

I got super-honest with myself and called my own bluff. I needed to set some goals. It is no more complicated than that. And then simply allow God to be in charge of the outcome.

One of my goals was to finish this book. And as you can see, we are getting really close! There were other things, like enjoying the life I have right now, helping others to do the same and not losing myself in the process. I am happy to say that all those things are actually happening right now.

If you have lost yourself in the busyness of today and have not considered why or how you are doing what you are doing...I dare you to stop and prayerfully consider the following questions:

1. What do you see yourself doing 10 years from now?
2. Are your daily activities supporting what you will be doing 10 years from nm now?
3. What can you do *today* that will get you closer to your goal?

Day 6 - It Doesn't Matter if You Aren't the Fastest!

I have been running for over 40 years. Yes, I do mean *literally*. I have heard from some non-runners that they tried running and hated it, and to them, all runs feel like they go on for 40 days and 40 nights. But that is not what I mean. I have been a runner for every bit of 40 actual years.

I love it for the sake of it. I love it for the feeling I get after I am done, and I love that at my age, I can still keep up with my kids! Let's be clear though, in all my years of running, I have rarely been the fastest. Well, okay, maybe in my age class. And well-after I stopped caring how I placed. There certainly are races now when I get left behind, but have to give myself kudos that I am still out there and happy to do it.

The longer I run, the more I love it and the more I love it, the more people I attract to it. The more people I attract to it, the more fit and healthy my town is and the more fit and healthy my town is, well...You can see where this is going, right?

Running well is not about always being the fastest. Sometimes, it is about having a smile on your face as your run. It is sometimes about sharing time with your friends and encouraging them to do their best, to not give up. For me, it is very much about running with my kids and my dog. It is also about becoming tougher and stronger for the hard stuff of life.

While I know that you can do this is any sport that pushes you beyond your limits, somehow, it seems that running will whip you into shape faster than anything. And, let's get real, if you can lay down a few miles when the temperatures are scorching and the humidity is soaring, you can do virtually anything.

I will run today because it makes me stronger, I will run today, because I know that I can. I will run because it will make me more able to do the hard stuff in my life tomorrow. I probably won't be the fastest, and that's okay.

1. What is the one hard thing you can do today that will make tomorrow easier?
2. How can you fit that into your schedule more often?
3. Do you have an accountability partner that can join you? Or maybe a group? If not, make a note in your journal or on your schedule so that you can track your progress...You are worth the effort! Even if you aren't the fastest.

Day 7 - All or None?

My tendency is to be very all-or-none. If I can't go full force, headlong into things, I catch myself avoiding doing anything at all. So instead, I tend to binge work, work too hard, work so long and with so much ferocity, that I wear myself out. This leads to the need for the inevitable and necessary: binge-break. That is, when I need a break so badly that I simply can't get myself to get back to it. Not a great strategy. It seems, there just has to be a better way.

Just like when you eat a delicious meal, one savory bite at a time, the experience is infinitely better than scarfing something at a traffic light in between practices. Likewise, I know that I have way more fun when I take a step back and relax into my work tasks, instead of forcing the work, when I am exhausted, frustrated or flabbergasted. Work literally works better when I savor it. Yes, savor it.

I am starting to see that the key to enjoying every minute, might simply be, to actually enjoy every minute. I think we tend to over-complicate this. A very necessary part of life is work, and if we want to enjoy life, then we need to train our brains to enjoy work. Even if you genuinely love what you do, there are bound to be things within your work-life that are not only not fun, but actually quite terrible to deal with. This is totally normal. We can train ourselves to enjoy even that, for the sake of the progress we are making. That is, if we are totally committed to staying in the game.

I'm talking about training ourselves to enjoy working for its own sake. History has proven to us that we are better humans when we are committed to a cause. We often function at the highest level when we have something to shoot for.

Today, I challenge you to think of all the good that you are bringing to the world in your dailyness. I want you to think about how being devoted to your cause brings out the best in you. Give yourself some kudos for how you have stayed in your game.

1. How have you sabotaged yourself, in the past, by quitting?
2. How can you ensure that you don't do it again?
3. What are you doing today that will take you in the direction of your dreams?

Don't Stop...

When something we do starts working, we often stop doing that very thing. We start losing weight or doing weights or making more money, we like what we see, and we pat ourselves on the back, we get complacent and let all the good disciplines slide. There is nothing inherently wrong with taking a short break. That can be healthy, necessary even. But when the break becomes so consuming that it over-rides our desire to get back into the game, that's a problem.

Perhaps a better way to think about your work life is to think in terms of calling. To realize that you are never really separate from it. This is not to say that you have to work *constantly*. There is nothing wrong with breaks or vacations. But learning to enjoy the journey, the toil and the failures, along with the successes. This just might be the key to prolonged satisfaction in your life. We must learn to stay in it, no matter what.

Here are a few reasons to love your work. For the sake of the service you are providing. Whether you are directly helping people, laying bricks, cooking a meal, or landscaping, there is an aspect of service built in. And that, my friend, is always worth it. Your contribution is leaving the world and your fellow man better off, because of your service. This is always worth the effort. The second reason, is that you have a chance to become a better person.

The skills you are using, the muscles you are building, the fortitude that it takes...these are all worth the effort. Your character will be stronger, when you get to work and even stronger when you stay there. As you persevere, your character is shaped and molded further. There is a special maturing that happens, as you quite literally come into your own. There is really no downside.

The third reason is that you learn to *believe in yourself*. You learn to trust yourself and you learn how not to be at the effect of the world around you. You show yourself that you can go to work and contribute,. You show yourself you can put your house in order. You show yourself that you have the ability to help and that no matter what happens, you have valuable and marketable skills. All of this is tremendously empowering.

Even as we develop all these skills and successfully navigate our work-life, it is critical that we realize that our calling *is* who we are. Every aspect of our lives either supports our calling or sucks the life out of it. Every time we give in to something other than our calling, we risk losing a bit of our best self. And the more frequently we give in to the time drainers, the more we dilute our calling.

Every day, we get to choose consciously to support our calling. Or we can unconsciously coast along and choose the things that don't support it. Unfortunately, the involuntary unconsciousness of not supporting our calling tends to catch us off-guard. We sort of fall into it. It is totally unexpected. Unintended.

You do this enough and you risk losing your intended consciousness *for good*. You do it enough and you will lose the ability to even come back to your calling....the ability to come back to the things that you love and the things that matter the most to you.

Here's what I want to offer. What if we could actually learn to enjoy our work? Our game? So much so, that we don't feel the need to escape or have the need to get away. If we commit to not stopping until it is time to move on to something else, or even better when we are actually done, then we will enjoy the break that much more.

Sticking with something until the task is done, provides a measure of clarity and simplicity that may not come any other way. Unfinished business tends to bog us down and makes us less efficient. The excess baggage clutters our brain, interfering with effective thinking. When we quit before we are done, with even the smallest of tasks, it gives us a sort of permission or tolerance, to quit at anything. And when we do that, we may never learn to stay in any game. We will get skilled at giving up at the least amount of resistance or discomfort.

Let's stop fostering the idea that work is work and *not working* is somehow better. Our work is our contribution to the world. It actually might be the most important thing that we do. Quitting before you are done, does way more harm in the long run, than the temporary relief you gain by quitting.

The muscles you grow from sticking with the hard stuff and grinding it out in the trenches will be invaluable when you get to the other side of hard. There is simply no way around the hard stuff, so work your way through it and know that you are held., every step of the way...

All you need to do is Stay in the Game.

Dr. Laura has been a practicing chiropractor since 1993. Together with her husband, Dr. Robert Sparks, they have stayed in the game for almost 30 years.

She is an avid runner, reader and mom of two teenagers. She would love to connect with you and hear how you are *staying in your game*. You can find her on Facebook at Dr Laura Sparks, on her website at www.drlaurasparks.com or by tuning into the Love Your Fit podcast.

This is her second book.

www.ingramcontent.com/pod-product-compliance
Lightning Source LLC
LaVergne TN
LVHW012020060526
838201LV00061B/4382